New Age

A Personal Testimony of
Two Kingdoms

Roy and Rae Livesey

New Wine Press

All quotations are from the Authorised Version Bible unless otherwise stated.
Scripture Quotations marked NIV are from the Holy Bible, New International Version.
Copyright © 1973, 1978, International Bible Society.
Published by Hodder & Stoughton.

New Wine Press,
PO Box 17,
Chichester. PO20 6YB
West Sussex,
England.

ISBN   0   947852   16   6

Printed and bound in Great Britain by
Anchor Brendon Ltd, Tiptree, Essex

To
Our Mothers,
Muriel Dean and Edith Livesey

Contents

Preface

Roy Livesey was a Chartered Accountant, Company Executive and businessman. By the world's standards he was successful – a nice wife and family, no real problems, a smart house and cash to spare for more or less anything the family wanted to buy.

Then he believed he faced financial disaster or even ruin. He worried for about a month; then a peace came upon him. Was it that peace which the world gives or was it 'that peace that passes all understanding'?

Spiritual Warfare was about to begin. He didn't know it. He had discovered the supernatural. He was entering the spiritual dimension where Jesus is found, but where also is found the counterfeit.

A course leading through nearly two years of extensive and painstaking 'search' must have seemed to deceiving spirits a good way to deal with a Chartered Accountant who had served pretty well up to this time without giving the 'evil one' too much difficulty! On a near full-time basis Roy was taken around this realm of spiritual power that he hadn't known existed.

At length God called a halt to Satan's wiles. Roy was given another big shock – this time a supernatural one – and he was drawn to Jesus. Then, baptised by the Holy Spirit, he was still in the spiritual dimension, but now he knew the infinite power of Jesus. The search had ended and it was time for discovery.

It was only when Roy came into the Kingdom of God that he became aware of having been in a kingdom before. He had come out of the Kingdom of Satan. On his conversion the Bible came alive to him, he could grasp its meaning, and he knew there were TWO KINGDOMS.

The expansion of occult activity, the focus on *discovering* the 'hidden mysteries' of the creation, and the focus on *protecting* the creation as we know it, has taken man's eyes off the Creator himself. Roy realised he had been part of a movement. It was the New Age Movement. It is not a recognisable organisation, but a movement of like-minded people networking together and pinning their hopes on what *they* can do, apart from God, focusing on one another, on peace, on protecting and discovering the creation for future generations, and getting involved in the occult realm.

The book is a PERSONAL STORY OF THE NEW AGE and of experiences gathered from involvement with the occult realm. It then shows how the supernatural is in every way better and more real when in the name of Jesus after the NEW BIRTH and not worked by demonic spirits who purpose to bring physical and spiritual death. Apart from showing Roy healings and miracles worked in His name, even more startling than he had witnessed before, the Lord, as the book testifies, took each of the areas of Roy's occult and New Age involvement giving him testimony upon testimony related to those areas and receiving the glory for Himself.

Except for a single chapter written by Rae, this is a book written for the most part in the first person singular by Roy. However it has been a joint effort. Roy has written the story from what have been his personal experiences, yet it has seemed right to present it together. Jesus said,

> 'Haven't you read, that at the beginning the Creator made them *male and female and said for this reason a man will leave his father and mother and be united to his wife, and the two will be one flesh?'*
> (Matthew 19: 4–5)

Both Roy and Rae are in the story together.

1

The Kingdom of Satan: Deception

I knew that John, living seventy miles away from me, was being alarmed by evil spirits. We knew one another well and we were both planning to set up as healers. We had attended the same training courses and I knew John was especially well gifted with psychic healing powers. Now John was unwell. Yet, more than that, I learned he was being tormented, chased around the room, by evil spirits.

We were both familiar with what we called the spirit world and with the idea that there were good spirits and bad spirits. John and I had been seeking to do good things with the powers we were discovering, and this was my first experience of evil powers coming on the scene. John had asked me to pray about these evil forces, and this I had been doing for several days.

Then I received a telephone call. I myself had been trying to contact John, but the call was to tell me John was dead.

The Sunday after John's death I chose to go to a 'Christian Spiritualist' church. I had been previously to a Spiritualist Church but never to a 'Christian Spirituralist' church. I wasn't a Christian so there was no way I could know that such a church was not Christian. I had a good regard for the Spiritualist Church I had been to, but had reached the position that it held no thrill any longer to see people receive messages, supposedly from the dead through a medium. They could show me nothing I hadn't seen

9

before! Yet I hadn't reckoned with the power of Satan; in this extremely run-down church, I was to hear from the spirit communication medium the most remarkable personal information I had yet received. As I set off to go there, it seemed fitting to the memory of John that I should choose a 'Christian' Church and a 'Spiritualist' Church. John reckoned to be a *Christian*; he had manifested *spiritual* powers.

Still I didn't know that *'Satan himself masquerades as an angel of light'*. (2 Corinthians 11:14). Satan knew me. Jesus knew me. They knew each other. Satan knew, as he knew since the Cross, that he was defeated in Heaven. But he was still very busy here on earth. This night he would put on his best show yet!

I was made very welcome at the 'Christian Spiritualist' church. The people there were very friendly. This particular evening was the occasion of the AGM. They were unable to hire the room other than for the Sunday meetings and so the business of the AGM had to be fitted into the time available. It became clear it was difficult to get a room to rent and people were unwilling to make the booking on discovering that it was for the Spiritualist Church.

After the election of the officers, and after consideration of the many matters traditionally found at an AGM, the President led the congregation in the singing of hymns. The President was a frail old lady and she next turned to the lady on her left who was badly crippled. She asked her if there were any 'messages'. I had consulted mediums in various places and this evening I felt resigned to a disappointing, dull and uneventful time, all rather dominated by an AGM. I must have been dulled by the AGM because I expected 'messages' to mean notices about weekly bingo or something like that! I should have known better.

Instead I was to witness the most accurate demonstration of clairvoyance I had yet seen, and *I* was to be the centre of attention. The lady opened with a person at the back of the room and apparently gave a very satisfactory message from the spirit 'guide'. By the standards I had come to know I judged this 'proof of survival' evidence to be very good indeed. The next subject on the other side of the room was also given a great deal of information about herself and she seemed very well satisfied too.

That was a lengthy demonstration and I expected the proceedings to close after two subjects. Then she said, 'I come now to the gentleman here at the front.' That was me! She looked for my nod of approval for her to continue and this was gladly given. I had never seen the medium before and I had travelled a good many miles to the meeting. My decision to go to this church rather than to any other was made only an hour or so before I set off. I write a good many letters and I had been writing many of a philosophical kind, including letters to John and my fellow-searchers. The medium started off with references to all my letter writing and then she said, 'Please, I want you to write a book. I want you to write a book because you *know*. You *know*.' She added, 'You believe in reincarnation.' I said, 'Yes, I do.' Had this lady put it to me a month previously I should have had to say I *didn't* believe in reincarnation. Now I believed that after death I would return to earth in another body. So she was on the ball right away!

Next the medium got on to my wife, Rae. Rae was not there with me. She was at home. 'She knows a lot too,' the medium said. 'I keep seeing a hand. They keep showing me a lovely hand. Your wife has seen this hand; perhaps in sleep state. Now this hand relates to another book,' she told me. 'You have been reading a book.' I signified that I was 'up to here in books', and that I had lately read so many! This was a very particular book, she said. She said it had a red cover. 'Not like your jumper; a *dark* red.' I thought about some of the books with red in the covers. 'No,' she said, 'this one is red all over. It's a lovely *leather* book.' That was it, I knew quite certainly which book it was. Had my wife been there she would have known too. But the lady went on, and without any help beyond my acknowledgement that she was correct. 'It's not a very big book. It has gold lettering. It has a gold embossed motif on the front – something like a prize. I'm inside the book now. They're showing me inside the front. The hand is showing me inside. It's a lovely book. Ask your wife about the hand. She will have seen the hand. It's a nice hand. There is an inscription in the front. It is in ink – real pen and ink. Do ask your wife about this. She will know all about it.' There was no doubt that I would do that! 'This will at last be something to interest her,' I thought. Rae had not taken kindly to my full-time search and I must have taken the thought straight out of Satan's own heart! 'I have the man here. He has been helping you. And I have the author. He will continue to help you. The hand signifies healing and teaching. He says you must never give the book away.'

Those are the most pertinent points I noted at the time; there was a great deal of supporting detail that summed up my own position and habits. It was easily the most impressive demonstration I had known. I could not have known that after that day I would never again go near a Spiritualist Church of any kind. As for the kindly lady giving the devil's information, I don't know whether she knew just how skilful the demons had been in selecting the material for her to give me.

During a break in the Christmas festivities I had been browsing amongst the old and ornamental leather-bound books that adorned the bookcase in the lounge of our home. They are the sort of books these days not considered very readable, and I had scarcely even noted any of the titles. That was no more than six weeks before the visit to the spiritualist meeting, and I had pulled out 'The Life of Jesus Christ' by Professor James Stalker, D.D. of Aberdeen. It was written in 1878 and there are 235 pages. Never before had I read such a book, and I read every word. Never before had I sat down with such an *old* book. It covered Jesus' healing ministry very thoroughly. As it seemed to me, it was relevant to my healing ideas, and I was pleased to understand Jesus' connection to what by this time I was getting near to doing!

It was after reading that book that I had gone each week one by one to the local churches. I had enthused over the book to my wife and tried to get her to read it. It was the healing I was interested in; the name of Jesus meant no more to me than another 'seal of approval' for all I was doing.

The medium had said 'write a book' and I don't believe that her deceiving spirit had such a book as *this* one in mind! She said 'don't ever give the leather book away'. I don't believe I shall!

'Don't ever give the book away. It is a very important book.' I imagine she would have given the name of the book had she been given it; but it might have been the nineteenth century equivalent of our 'porn' for all she knew. 'You are to read that book again and again,' she kept saying. What a clever way for Satan to heap credibility on his '*Christian* Spiritualist' establishment. What a perfect demonstration of the Biblical description of Satan masquerading as an Angel of Light!

'Your wife *knows*,' the medium kept telling me. '*You* will give her the confidence to bring it out.' When she spoke of 'knowing' she was referring to the truth. When I was talking afterwards with the medium she told me I was very advanced and had passed through very many incarnations. I had found that most in the world of the psychic and the occult had well-developed egos. Mine was fast moving that way too.

After a cup of tea and pleasantries all around, I couldn't wait to be off and tell my wife. I wanted her in this too. That was to be the way it was before bedtime! I told Rae the whole long story and got the book from the shelf. I hadn't noticed every detail before, but there it was: the red leather and gold, and the presentation label in the front, 'Presented by the Education Committee of the Staffordshire Church Schools Association to Mr William Wyborn of Wolstanton

C.E. School as a special recognition of faithful service rendered to the Church for 24 years – 31st May 1924'.

It was all quite easy to relate to my wife. She had been unimpressed by my pressure to read the book, but she was familiar with it as it was always left around to win her interest. She well remembered Mr Wyborn, who the medium believed was in communication with her. The hand made sense to Rae. From Mr Wyborn's visits in her childhood she remembered especially those nice hands with long fingers. He called on her grandmother regularly and was remembered as a rather awesome holy person standing for all that was reckoned to be good. No doubt she would have to be on her best behaviour when Mr Wyborn visited.

My wife's interest was won. The image of Mr Wyborn had been conjured, and off she went to the old photographs. Mr Wyborn was found, albeit in black and white. It showed big hands, hat, dog and my wife as a nine year old. The penny had dropped! Rae was on board! Satan must have been rubbing *his* big hands! Only a short time before, the large batch of photographs had arrived from Rae's family. Mr Wyborn's photograph – the only one of him – was on the top. Yet Satan, the evil one, was reckoning without God's plan and to that he has no access. My wife's interest in the occult was to last less than 24 hours. That compared to my 10 months, or 22 months counting from my intensive encounter with Moral Re-Armament.

The Lord was on the scene more or less immediately, to get my wife back on the straight-and-narrow. He used an ugly story that was to bring me back too.

The next day there was a call from another mutual friend, this time telling of the dreadful circumstances in which John's body was found. These were ugly, and not for relating in these pages. I did not see John for myself but the description of the wounds given to me was alarming indeed. I had been unable to contact him and I was told that foul play was suspected. The telephone was ripped out by police after a telephone call in which another mutual friend was involved. The police uncovered nothing to support their idea and I was left to conclude that the wounds were the climax of a week of torment and that they were self-inflicted. He died in the course of a terrible onslaught by demons just like the man with the unclean spirit among the tombs in Mark 5:5.

My wife was never one to feel much alarm, to lose any sleep, to suffer depressions or to take any tablets. But this news of the way John died caused her great alarm. She did on this occasion take the problem to bed. Immediately the Lord spoke to her. 'Trust me,' He said.

As for me I didn't know Jesus. I had been delving deep into Satan's territory. My materialistic 'do-gooding' New Age existence that had dominated my life, eventually led me into the occult realm. This was a shock that caused me to alter course. I had to make sure this wasn't going to happen to me.

2

Early Days as a New Ager

Excepting that the 1939-1945 war came right in the middle of my childhood, my young days could only be described as unexceptional. An only child, my parents were ambitious for me, and I soon carried on where they left off. I was ambitious for myself.

When the war ended I started to go to Sunday School at the Church of England nearest to where we lived, and I continued as a member of that church for twenty years. My recollections of that time are feint. I can remember scriptures I must have gathered there, but I never remember *hearing* the gospel, at least in any way that was meaningful to *me*.

Although only averagely bright, the main focus was always the schoolwork. I was a Grammar School boy. Even at that time I could see absolutely no relevance of what I was learning to the world outside. I can remember the subjects studied most clearly, and I can remember much of the content. They were a means to examination successes and certificates. Whilst then seeing them all as without purpose, I see them differently today. They were all in God's plan. We learned *not* Greek or Hebrew, the languages of the Bible, but Latin, the language of the Roman antichrist. In ancient history we covered in great detail the civilisation of Greece and the conquests of Rome; yet there was no Bible history. Certainly I remember no Bible study lessons. The modern history – we studied up to 1914 – could be substantially re-written given a fairer view of the facts. Later on, at university for my Economics Degree what I remember above all other things I was taught was that it was impossible to have unemployment *and* inflation at the same time. The world hasn't turned out that way!

Of course I didn't *know* Jesus. I didn't have a personal relationship with Him nor therefore could He be my Saviour and Lord. I didn't know Jesus was building His church, preparing His bride for the day of His return. I didn't know Satan was preparing his bride too. I didn't know Satan had got me involved very early on in what is today known as the New Age movement, a loose network of people and groups with a thread of thinking which focused them, without their knowing it, on ideas leading eventually to the occult realm and a one-world government ready to receive the antichrist when he appears in the flesh. The New Age is a big subject; the main thrust of the first part of this book concerns my progressive involvement in it, through 'good works' and eventually into the occult realm.

At university I became active in politics and quasi-political groups. At that time I was in the socialist camp and became Chairman of the Labour Party in the student body at Bristol. Also, and without knowing the significance then, I was active in the Student United Nations group where once again I became Chairman. Significantly too, I was attracted to the ideological movement called Moral Re-Armament (MRA). As I sought, through one means after another, to see what were the answers the world needed, I believed I had found them in the absolute moral standards that were the focus of MRA living. Like the United Nations, MRA was to be a significant part of my story. Some twenty odd years later I was to be alert to what is going on in the New Age. Chapter seventeen describes that new awareness.

As a young man I started off with an earnest aim for all the most acceptable qualifications, and by the age of 24 I was a Chartered Accountant with a University degree in

Economics and Government. My area of work was always in the field of commerce, finance or international trade. By the time I was 28 I was a senior executive in the British Motor Corporation Group, and an ambition-peak was reached when I was made a director of a small BMC company. After that came a much wider experience, both self-employed and as an executive of one company or another. Altogether there was a full twenty years in accountancy and economics. Most recently I had represented Arab principals in the United Kingdom. Previous to that, as Financial Manager of a very large company with substantial business in the Arab oil areas, I travelled a great deal in the Arab world.

I discovered the buzz word in conversations about the economies of the world. It was 'oil'. The Middle East was centre-stage and Satan had me on his side in that area too. Although I wasn't aware of it, I was anti-semitic as I pursued my commercial purposes in the Middle East. I was anti-semitic without even thinking about Jews.

Satan's purposes were served as I moved around the Muslim world joining with other westerners, unashamedly only there for the pay or the profit. Whatever the Arabs wanted, the westerners were there to supply it to them. The Arabs wanted every kind of service and supply. It was supplied and I was there weighing in my financial expertise regardless of the purpose.

In Saudi Arabia, the Muslim government demanded that the Christian God was not worshipped. That was the law. I was there in Riyadh one Friday watching a robber's hand cut off for stealing. The oil-rich governments demanded their suppliers didn't supply to Israel, and I was out there wiring to my principals the risks to their business if they didn't comply. Those risks were great indeed, in economic terms. Much depended on the business in Saudi Arabia and the Gulf. Whatever was God's *supernatural* purpose it was for me a *natural* decision to say 'no' to Israel.

There are many ways to say 'no'. I never thought about

18

Israel. I didn't have any relationships with Israelis to spark such thoughts. Had I stopped-over on one of my flights to see the home of God's chosen people and of Jesus himself, my passport would have been marked and I would not have been permitted easy access to do my business in the Muslim world. So instead I would 'stop over' in places like Cairo to see the pyramids, or at Baalbeck in Lebanon where I visited the temple of Baal! Thus I said 'no' to Israel. I didn't think about it until I became a Christian, but I was involved just the same.

The Arabs and the rest of us were destroying Israel economically. And if we didn't stick to that policy, then the Arabs could destroy *our* economy. Arab oil has for a long time now been converting into cash. Muslim influence is measured in terms of oil *and* money. Israel, and many other nations too, were being greatly damaged by the economic battle that was raging. It is in the economics that we find the hearts of men and of nations. Only as a Christian could I see the waste and despair that is spread by the international dealings of the conglomerate corporations. Only as a Christian could I see the evil that permeates the business and economic scene in all its aspects. Mine was a part in all of that.

3

The Touch of God?

The first night away in London I lay in my bed; something very different had happened to me. The full significance of my experience was not to dawn for many months. But life thereafter would be different – very different indeed.

I was spending a long weekend away with my family. There was my wife Rae and children, Sue aged 14 and David who was 12. We also had with us a young French visitor. Our declared purpose was to show London to her, but we were all glad of the weekend away. For me in particular, things at home had been especially trying. I was getting away from it all or recharging my batteries. As it turned out it was to be very much more than that.

In that summer I didn't know Jesus. I had heard that God is known to speak to people when they are down. I was down alright! Then, for reasons I could not explain, I was to find peace. It was very sudden. It was as if a burden was lifted.

The change had started earlier in the day on the train journey from New Street, Birmingham to London, Euston. I had made that journey many times in the past both as a company executive and as a private businessman. Never did I work on the journey in the manner of so many of my colleagues. I used to reckon this was a time for reflection, for getting the ideas, and hopefully for getting a bit of inspiration.

On this extraordinary journey my idea was: 'don't worry!' Many people had said this many times; I must have said it, or thought it, as frequently as most. Doing something about it was always quite another matter. But this time was different. I couldn't explain things, but it was as if I was being helped. I hadn't prayed in years. I was being helped in a way I neither understood nor questioned. By the time we arrived at Euston I had concluded I would not be worrying any more. There was real conviction in the resolve.

My problem had been a financial one. I rarely lacked confidence in the area of personal finance. I had always spent a great deal of money, and always I had been able to earn more than enough. With sound business deals, and investment, I had seen my capital grow. As I decided upon the trip to London, and even as I boarded the train, all this seemed threatened. The threat had been hanging over the family for about a month. As the man with the figures, the head of the family, and a Chartered Accountant into the bargain, my load seemed particularly heavy.

The middle of 1980 was a financially difficult time for many. My own business was no exception. With appropriate caution I was running down the scale of operation. But there was another and more significant financial factor. A great deal of my capital had come from watching the value of my assets increase. We lived in a village called Walborough for nine years and were moving away to another large house where there was more land for the family's horses. Also there would be considerable cash to spare after the sale at Walborough, which would have provided a nice cash injection for my various business activities or for producing a good investment income.

We had committed ourselves to this *before* selling the house we occupied and this financial burden amounted to a great deal of money. We were looking for a good price on our existing property but bank interest rates were set to rise to 21% for the sort of bridging loan that we had. After this financial point-of-no-return had been reached I made a calculation to see at what point I would be reduced to bankruptcy, at least if the house remained unsold. Our comfortable lives and security were all threatened.

'Money is the root of all evil'. I never regarded that statement as one of the more profound truths and I didn't know I was misquoting the Bible; it was, however, one of the sayings that had floated through my mind many times over many years. On that train in 1980 I was still a long way from even picking up a Bible. I had heard about it being easier for a camel to go through the eye of a needle than for a rich man to enter the Kingdom of Heaven! My thought on that train was that money was just not worth all the hassle. Why *should* I worry; it would probably be a good thing for me if I were to go bust! I reflected, as I often had, that life had always been pretty consistent with no very serious ups and downs. We had always been reasonably contented.

I recalled the relevance of money in my life. It had always *seemed* important. I had always spent plenty of it and, more significantly, I had more and more as the years moved on. This was the way so common in the 1960s and 1970s in the Western world, and in material terms we had a great deal to reckon. I considered myself fortunate that I had had no terrible problems in my life, apart from a fairly serious motor accident soon after moving to our house in Walborough. I didn't know Jesus had a plan for me. I didn't know Satan had power too, nor did I know I was well focused in his sights.

However that one hour and thirty-five minutes on the train to London was not a time packed with thoughts and ideas. It was a time that I recall for the dawn of a new peace. The simple thought that money had never made any difference to the level of real joy seemed to prompt a peace. I had thought it with my mind on so many occasions. But my heart was now receiving the proposition. Life would never be the same again. As Jack Mowate, a clergyman friend was to say to me many months later, God had put his finger on me. Yet I had much to experience before I would *know* Him.

After a pleasant evening with our hosts it was time for bed and to be alone with these new thoughts. Usually bed-time would provide the opportunity for all the fears to return, a little tossing and turning might have been expected, and quite certainly I should have awakened at about five o'clock to resume worrying until it was time to get up. There was no tossing and turning. I was filled with a new joy. I did very little thinking, and certainly no worrying. I was awake until four o'clock when I fell soundly asleep. I had enjoyed being awake until that late hour. I was simply relaxed and enjoying this new situation. I felt good when I got up the next morning. Again untypically, I did not suffer at all from lack of sleep. The morning was different. I was different. Any sort of tentative assessment of my new condition was now in the past. Something *had* happened. I was now in a different ball-park! I couldn't have explained it and I didn't try. I simply said to my wife how good I was feeling that morning. I had been down and now I wasn't depressed at all. I could never have expected the prospect of a few days sightseeing in London to lift my human spirit in such a way!

The journey and my night with the new-found peace had been quite extraordinary.

4

Meeting Moral Re-Armament An Encounter After 19 years

After a leisurely Thursday morning about the house with our hosts we were headed for Buckingham Palace and the Royal Mews. That was the plan for the afternoon. It would take us into the centre of sightseers' London; and Odile, with us from France, would surely want to see Trafalgar Square, the Houses of Parliament and all the rest in the Buckingham Palace area. It was agreed that at the opening time of 2.15 p.m. we would see the gold State Coach, the horses and other ceremonial coaches in the Royal Mews.

We stood in the queue which stretched along Buckingham Palace Road. At once my eyes caught sight of the big display sign outside the Westminster Theatre. There it was, 'WESTMINSTER THEATRE'. I immediately recalled the significance of that theatre. The last time I had anything to do with Moral Re-Armament was there. The theatre was the Headquarters of the movement I had known at University – Moral Re-Armament (MRA).

I gazed at the sign and as the queue moved forward I could not leave my thoughts behind. I excused myself and was off to the Westminster Theatre. 'I'll just go and have a look at what I can find. I'll join you in the Mews very soon,' I told the others.

Out of the sunlight I walked off down the shadowed side street only stopping briefly when I spotted a brass plate on a

24

side door. It read 'Oxford Group – Registered Office'. That spoke to me and I was thrilled that the Oxford Group, which had given birth to the idea of MRA was still in being. MRA was alive and well. The theatre was spick and span just as I remembered everything in MRA. The theatre still belonged to them.

Nineteen years earlier I ended my connection with MRA, and the last event I attended was a production of 'The Ladder' at the Westminster Theatre. This was the story of a man climbing the ladder of so-called success. Just out of University, and in spite of the play, I was then about to start my own climb in search of success. Now back at the Westminster Theatre, I had been up the ladder; in fact I was on my way down again.

I remembered Frank Buchman, the Founder of MRA, had died in the summer of 1961. I was in West Africa at the time and I had written a letter in the 'Ashanti Pioneer'. This was the leading daily paper of the Ashanti region of Ghana and they printed my letter by way of an obituary. The reception of the idea of Moral Re-Armament in Britain had been mixed, and opponents lined up for a variety of reasons. I had found the reception of the idea overseas to be better. Peter Howard's book (written with Dr Paul Campbell from America), 'Remaking Men', was always on my shelf; and more than any other book, this set out how *I* thought life ought to be lived. It was my 'bible'; and I *did* read it from time to time. I had been a supporter of Moral Re-Armament ever since being canvassed when chairman of the University Labour Party. I was very much against the main stream in giving MRA my support. I had never put MRA completely out of my mind.

As I climbed the steps of the theatre it was evident that Peter Howard had succeeded Frank Buchman as leader. Howard had also died and the big memorial stone could not be missed. That theatre foyer was very welcoming. It felt good. It was comfortable. People were all smiles and kindness. All were quite obviously welcome. You could buy food and a cup of coffee without the feeling that it was a business transaction! People wanted to serve you, and it was a good feeling.

In the corner of the foyer there was a book-stall. Surely enough I could still buy 'Remaking Men'. I could still buy 'Remaking the World', something of a standard work for MRA and containing the speeches of Frank Buchman. I had never been a big reader of books and the only ones I had ever bought in any number were from MRA during 1960-1961. Here I was, within twenty-four hours of my new peace, face to face once again with MRA. I bought many books, a large number by any standard. It would have seemed a very large number to the salesman, particularly after I had shared my financial plight with him!

That was later in the afternoon. I knew I would want much time with him and with these exciting new book titles. It seemed even in the titles themselves there was much to help and inspire. I excused myself and said I would surely return with my family in an hour, and I ran back the hundred yards or so to the Royal Mews.

How would my wife Rae like to be drawn into this excitement? Really I didn't know the answer and maybe she would see it as an irksome distraction from day's plan. I imagined she would expect me to be talking, leaving her bored and the children at a loose end. Anyway after the tour of the horses and carriages they would at least perhaps be ready for a rest and a cup of coffee. Quite willingly all came along to the Westminster Theatre. My wife could not fail to sense the welcoming atmosphere of the place. The salesman talked easily and honestly to all of us. All the family liked him and it is not surprising at all that he became a family friend. He seemed easily able to identify with all of us. Moral Re-Armament was working just as I remembered it. Typical of testimonies I had heard nineteen years before, he shared with me his story of repaying postage stamps wrongly taken from a previous employer. I believe we were all up-lifted by that meeting with this young man. He cared about all of us individually; there would be no doubt that we would see him again. This was the first of a new sort of relationship.

What is Moral Re-Armament? I didn't know all of the answer to that one. I *thought* I did; I knew pretty well about people who were in MRA. Nothing I read or was told in 1980 was any different from what I had understood in 1960. But I didn't know Jesus; this was also a big shortcoming in the MRA idea, but of course it escaped my notice. Moral Re-Armament looked liked the answer for me. What a remarkable coincidence! So soon after my experience on the train, 'God' comes along and gives me some support for my new situation! That is how it seemed then.

The people I had known in MRA sought to live their lives along the lines of four absolute moral standards. These are absolute honesty, absolute purity, absolute love and absolute unselfishness. The quiet time for guidance early each morning is central to the MRA idea, and during this period you write down your thoughts and ideas for the day. They have to be consistent with these standards and if, on that basis, they are found to be not 'of God', then they have to be set aside.

My story is one of exposing the occult, the cults and false religious movements; my later search from 1980 to 1982, took me into a great number of very dangerous areas. I believed I knew a great deal about cults and the occult by the middle of 1982, after coming to know Jesus. If experience was anything to go by it could have been presumed I knew much about these subjects. Yet it was not until much later that God was to speak to me also about the subtle dangers of the religious movement – or cult – I knew best: Moral Re-Armament. It might have been Rosicrucianism or Freemasonry. I might have been a Jehovahs Witness or a Mormon. My experience was of Moral Re-Armament.

The list of cults is endless with more and more being added every month. The occult scene becomes more and more of interest to the growing numbers who are searching. It would be easy to argue that Moral Re-Armament is not as bad as the rest in any list. Jesus would not look at it that way I am quite sure. There is only one truth and anything else is not truth. When I first met my pastor he told me 'I am 35 years old. If I told you I was 34, it would be nearly true but I would be deceiving you.' So it is with Moral Re-Armament.

What attracted me to Moral Re-Armament in 1960? I was a Chartered Accountant. As I didn't see myself specialising in this area I had gone to university in Bristol to read Economics and Politics. It was the activities outside the curriculum that most interested me. Politics, economics, business, international affairs – all of these areas took some of my time. I had wanted to put the world to rights – not an uncommon idea with students of any generation. I was 23 years old, and I had come to the conclusion the world would never be put right – certainly not with any of the ideas I had come across. Then a group from Moral Re-Armament arrived in Bristol. The university area of the city seemed to be full of people with the message of Moral Re-Armament. They were a group of pleasant people and their absolute standards seemed to show through in the way they lived their lives. Their message was good too; or so it seemed at that time. MRA taught me that the quality of man is reflected in the quality of Government. Men had to change, then governments would be changed. MRA worked directly at changing the men in governments and in leadership positions.

I learned a great deal whilst I was off on this MRA tangent. In spite of being a member of my Anglican church, I never did have my roots anchored in Jesus in those days. Yet I do wonder how I might have moved nearer to Jesus but for MRA. I didn't have a Bible. I reckoned it too ponderous and difficult. But did 'Remaking Men' by Campbell and Howard keep me in the world of the Humanists? I believe it must have helped. 'Remaking Men' conveniently spelled out for me the things I already felt in my bones, the things I had been brought up to believe and a few rather obvious things that in one way or another would escape the attention of a self-interested student. I have said I regarded the book as my bible. That is my fault, it can be argued. Such is the likely effect of the book on many; and off they go at a tangent. I did not know the power of Jesus until 22 years later. When I re-met MRA in 1980 it is clear, from a letter I wrote to the young book salesman shortly afterwards, that I still had the basic problem. I wrote 'So how does one keep to the path?' How *do* you live according to these exacting standards in your own strength? Some people can do some remarkable things in their own strength. Some are even a stone's throw away from doing some remarkable things with the evil power of Satan masquerading as the Bible warns, as an angel of light. I was to pass that way myself. Cults focus on human strengths and discipline; the formula or technique takes the place of the living relationship with Jesus. The way of the cults is self-effort, and that leads, however subtly, to the old lie of the serpent that we can be like God. 'Ye are gods' is what is eventually whispered in our ears.

There is no doubt that MRA tuned up my human strengths and spirit over those years, and when I turned to my books on MRA – new and old – following that exciting day in London, I could easily see how my life had been changed by Moral Re-Armament. It was both exciting and encouraging to reflect on the specific ways my life had run on MRA lines. I even found in the books quotations that I had been giving people over the years without realising where I got them. Happily, I find myself now quoting Bible texts from my youth!

But Moral Re-armament *does* change men. I had heard of many examples in 1960. I believe too that MRA has had its successes in turning history. All of us who had anything to do with MRA were familiar with the role played by Frank Buchman in bringing together Conrad Adenauer and

Robert Schuman for the first time after the 1939–45 war. I have never had any reason to doubt this, nor indeed to doubt this was a significant factor in the remarkable reconciliation of France and Germany. I am familiar with other 'successes' of this kind, and there are very many. No-one could, I believe, doubt the effectiveness of particular initiatives under the umbrella of Moral Re-Armament. Initiatives involve men and women, and I believe there are many well-intentioned people at work within Moral Re-Armament. The danger, I was to discover, was with an idea that touches upon morals and religion without being Jesus-centred.

I was not aware of the spiritual dimension when I met MRA either in 1960 or in 1980. The following extract from 'Remaking Men' sets out the alternatives; without reckoning the primacy of the power of Jesus, nor the power of Satan working through the numerous religions that come together in MRA:

'But Moral Re-Armament is not another activity. It is a way of life. It is the way to do what needs to be done. It makes clear the priorities in life and releases a man from slavery to multitudinous activities which even when achieved do not solve the problems. The materialistic forces advance not by the strength of their ideas but by the absence from the field of any other world idea compellingly lived. A passionate pursuit of evil can be met only by a passionate pursuit of good. The plans of ruthless men to dominate the world can be met only by men committed to bringing the ideology of change and unity to their communities and nations. The chips are down. It is organised materialism for the nations or Moral Re-Armament. It is for us to choose. Our decision will determine the future.'*

There is some sense in all of that, but without Jesus it is a deception, and one of those tangents to divert people from the real thing. With people in MRA who don't know Jesus the error is understandable; they may be kept from knowing Him.

*Remaking Men' by Dr Paul Campbell and Peter Howard (Blandford Press, Poole, Dorset, England)

me then. But now I am looking as a Christian. Without that wonderful power of the Holy Spirit I don't believe that the motion passed by the Church Assembly on the Report would have meant anything to me. It was passed in the following form:

'The Assembly having received and considered the Report prepared by the Social and Industrial Council on the movement known as MRA, does not desire to record any judgments either upon the merits or upon the demerits of this movement, remembering that every church and every movement stands always under the judgment of Almighty God. It prays that all Christian people may humbly seek in all that they do to know more clearly the mind of Christ the Lord and to obey more faithfully the will of the Holy Spirit, that God may in all things be glorified.'

I have read the pages of the debate on the Report where I find the individual opinions.

I do not seek to judge any supporter of the movement whether he be a professing Christian or a Hindu. *But do look at the movement.*

Moral Re-Armament provided the standard for my life for more than twenty years. It was only after careful reflection that I see this is so. Of course I failed miserably against those standards of absolute honesty, absolute purity, absolute love and absolute unselfishness. But these *were* the standards. MRA was the *basis* for my life because I did *try* to apply them.

In 1980, and exhilarated by the friendships that came from the meeting at the Westminster Theatre, I still hadn't done all my homework on MRA. More particularly God had not spoken to me about it. I did not yet know Jesus. I believed my problem for twenty years had been materialism and the absence of Moral Re-Armament. Rather my problem had been materialism *plus* Moral Re-Armament, but I felt on top of the world.

I never experienced 'pushiness' from people working

with MRA. The man at the bookstall was a quiet man and, to me, he seemed admirable in every way. Excited about MRA I was determined to keep contact with him and two days after first meeting him in the theatre I dropped him a line. These are some of the things I said:

> What a coincidence, if that is what it was (!), to be waiting in the queue for the Royal Mews and to see the sign 'Westminster Theatre'.
>
> I think I had started to face things more sensibly within 24 hours *before* seeing that sign. That is the strange thing! Perhaps the effects are usually and more normally within 24 hours *after* your help.
>
> That doesn't in any way diminish the great value of your help – the fertiliser rather than the seed perhaps in this case'?
>
> I don't think I ever really doubted the rightness and good sense of MRA – unlike many in the class of 1961! Nonetheless to re-enter the Westminster Theatre and to meet you in 1980, and to find that both it, and people like I met in Bristol in 1960, are alive and well, was reassurance indeed.

I was so excited I couldn't wait for a reply, and three days later I wrote to him again. It was in this one that I posed the question 'so how does one keep to the path?' I didn't know it, but that's where Jesus was needed.

He replied with a letter that encouraged me. He said he would now be able to ask more knowingly in prayer for the best to happen to me and my family. He urged me to keep to the decision of waiting upon God particularly first thing in the morning. A good relationship was just beginning with this young man, and I could not have then realised that new relationships with literally dozens of friends would flow from it. Things started to get better on the financial front. More than ever now aware of what I was calling coincidences, it seemed significant that I was visiting an MRA home and conference centre when I learned that sale details had been agreed for my house. The financial problem that had brought me to the difficulty was getting sorted out. I remember thinking how significant it was that I learned of the sale agreement whilst I was actually at the centre. We had been invited to go there for the day, and prior to what I called my experience on the train I would have cancelled anything to remain at home on that day to arrange these most important house sale details in a personal way. As it was I was happy to leave all to my solicitor, and all I had to do was telephone him from the centre in the afternoon.

I believe that some of the other new relationships in MRA were a help too. Any group of people constitutes a 'mixed bunch'. A couple with whom Rae and I became especially well acquainted were farmers living close by. They had worked with MRA for many years and at various times they had worked full time. I thought of this couple as good examples living lives on the basis of the four absolute standards. I liked to share what I was thinking and to get their views. We spent many a long hour together through the winter of 1980/1981. Our sessions together would end with a time of 'guidance' when we listened to see what God was saying. We read the Bible together. Of course I had heard the Bible read in church; from time to time in the distant past I must have read bits of it too. Yet I couldn't remember when! I found it very heavy going, a tiresome struggle and very difficult indeed.

The year 1981 was to be eventful. I resolved this would be a year when I would, in the modern parlance 'get it all together'. I could not have been more wrong.

5

MRA at Caux:
Where the Religions Meet

When I reported to my wife on my 3½ weeks of conferences and courses in the summer of 1981, I said it was a most stimulating and exciting time. It was all so remarkable I didn't believe it would be possible to convey any sort of true understanding of my experience. My first stop had been the MRA Conference Centre at Caux in Switzerland where I spent 2½ weeks.

I left Switzerland in the belief *that* experience could never be matched anywhere. My wife had the opportunity to come. She loves Switzerland, but the Holy Spirit kept her away and she declined. Now I am glad she did. Like the more widely-known Freemasonry, Moral Re-Armament is an open-house to the world's religions. They meet at Caux.

I was met at Caux railway station by Ralph. I knew Ralph in 1960-61 when we were both students in Bristol. Now he was working full-time for MRA in America. The usual 'coincidences' had already been at work prior to this rendezvous in Caux. Ralph and his wife were holidaying in Somerset just three weeks before. This was their first visit to England in four years; we were holidaying in Somerset at the same time. We were able to have an enjoyable family day together. Our wives got to know one another for the first time.

The Caux Conference Centre is a magnificent place high up in the mountains overlooking the lake above the town of

Montreux. The scenery is idyllic. The accommodation is grand and well appointed. I very easily slipped into relationships with all kinds of people. My single room was in the adjacent Grand Hotel, an establishment that previously belonged to MRA. It was now run by the Rosicrucians. I had still to learn that the Rosicrucians were another cult. The weather was perfect. There was a pleasurable routine and the MRA centre ran on the trust that those attending would do the work. After a day there, I was perfectly happy to sign on for the team waiting at the table and washing up, and I found myself working alongside a British Member of Parliament.

I was lined up for a big plateful of MRA. I was there for three conferences. Some had been there much longer and would stay longer still. I looked forward to the conference on Industry, but it was the Africa conference that interested me especially. The third conference I attended was the Political conference.

In the conference debates I saw no evidence that supported the 1955 position seen in the Report of the Church Assembly; MRA appeared to take the nature of politics seriously. Indeed there was ample evidence to me at Caux that many of those engaged on the political scene, in the unions, in management or in a more central political area, are fully aware of what they are about. They are in the business of getting men to be honest, unselfish, loving and pure, and in an absolute sort of way. There was ample testimony to the success of the initiatives. These were both behind the scenes and on the conference floor. There could be seen bridge building and reconciliation.

Clearly some delegations had been sponsored for the trip to Caux. Others were there because they had been before and wouldn't miss any opportunity when they could afford it if they believed it was right to go. It struck me that the greatest value was to those taken out of the turmoil of affairs in their own government or trade union or whatever. Problems could be seen in a different light.

There were to be found at Caux some very well disciplined individuals. I could not fail to be impressed by the ex-Mau Mau leader who was on the conference platform with a white woman. Thirty years previously he had been responsible for the burial-alive of the woman's father, a rich White Highland farmer in Kenya. There had been forgiveness and they had become friends. I was impressed too when I heard a former cabinet minister of an African country declare how people had come from Europe with bribes to get business. One of them, he said, was for 'a million dollars – paid anywhere' and he had refused it. I was impressed when a former British Ambassador spoke by way of apology on behalf of the British people. 'I know that million dollars was offered by a British company', he said. In my own business life I had come across much that was corrupt, and neither the ambassador's comments nor the amount involved were any surprise to me. As a financial executive in big companies it had been my unhappy duty to root out corruption where I had found it. I had done so and been caused not a few personal problems along the way.

I could readily identify with the cabinet minister. Perhaps he was a loner doing what he had believed to be right; like me he was finding some like-minds in MRA.

As I sat back in the luxurious surroundings of the conference I could see my own situation reflected in the matters shared on bribery and corruption. I opened my heart to those I had hurt with my investigations of bribery and corruption. I sat down and wrote letters of apology for those hurts, and in response to my own guilt. I knew there was someting for me in the cabinet minister's message; yet I was still reckoning without Jesus. It was self-righteousness.

I do not judge any of the lovely people there at Caux. I am sure many were searching just as I was. The tragedy is to believe the answer can be found at Caux, elsewhere in MRA or in any place that, knowingly or otherwise, by-passes the cross of Calvary. I was impressed by that African cabinet minister. I hope he too has discovered Jesus in a personal way. Other African leaders brought to the conference were impressed too. I believe many will have been sparked to some change in their own lives. Yet, as the Church Assembly Report put it in 1955, the MRA view of change is less than the Christian view of conversion.

One man was the leader of the Liberal Party in a Southern African country. He shared with me the changes he was going to bring about in his party on the basis of the 'guidance' he had received at Caux. For my own part I still had a role in British Liberal politics. I had been a constituency chairman for three years, and on the basis of my 'guidance' at Caux I drafted and organised the printing of one thousand leaflets for distribution at our Llandudno Liberal Party Assembly. My leaflet followed the theme of the Political conference at Caux and it had special relevance to the working of the new Liberal-S.D.P. Alliance to be cemented at that Assembly. I wish that Caux were nothing more than a place for good political initiatives. That Liberal Assembly message was, I believe, the nearest I ever came to offering – however vaguely – any sort of solution during 25 years of interest in British politics; it may even be that it contributed to the excellent temper in debate that was a particular feature of that Assembly.

At Caux the number of parliamentarians and members of government seemed endless. They came from all over the world. There was an African President, a Roman Catholic Archbishop, a deposed King and Queen recently returned from the Charles and Diana Royal Wedding. The occasion was a feast for name-droppers! MRA is criticised because its people aim high to get things changed. Yet that was practical politics as I understood it.

The Holy Spirit hadn't of course made me sensitive to the dangerous *religious* aspect of MRA with its acceptance of all religions and its zealous focus on self. I am sure the same can be said for other visitors, but I doubt that they left with only some simple *political* lesson! I couldn't then speak on behalf of Jesus. I was not at all offended by the enormous

41

mural which was said to incorporate various religions in its design. Today it would be different. In spite of benefits the risk and danger is great. My call to Christians is to pray for those in Moral Re-Armament and to speak out as the Holy Spirit leads to present the Christian assessment of the movement. What value are a few solutions of the human spirit in this life when the price is encouraging people to miss the life with Jesus in the next one? What price on denying Jesus Christ as the Son of God and not using such an international forum to signal the way to eternal life?

When I arrived at Caux I was enlisted to take a part in a stage production of 'The Ladder'. I was given a copy of the play and there I could read, 'The Ladder was produced at the Westminster Theatre, London, opening on 25th October 1961 . . .' I had been there. It was the last event of MRA I had attended. Now here I was, twenty years later, and *appearing* in the play. Another coincidence, or just another reminder that I had missed the point of the play as a young man? It was good fun to do. A former Hollywood actress I had met with MRA in Bristol was its competent producer; my friend Ralph played a leading part. I didn't know that in God's plan nothing was a coincidence. The play was nothing but good, *and* with a Christian basis. Yet still I suggest that association with MRA is like stroking a tiger's tail when the tiger is asleep. Carry on for long enough and you are in trouble! It took me 22 years to see it. How can I talk piously to my Hindu friends about absolute standards, and not tell them about Jesus who was the same 2000 years ago, today and forever (Hebrews 13: 8)? How can I compromise on the truth that whoever doesn't believe in Him, who is God's own Son, can't have God the Father either (1 John 2: 23)?

After the MRA conferences it was still only my intellect at work. My heart was still not moving. I did not know that Satan is the ruler on this earth and that God allows this in working out His purposes in us according to His plan. Now I know that with my heart. I could never have seen it with my intellect.

42

Certainly many of my weak spots were touched through MRA, particularly during that intensive time of conference, fellowship and sharing in Switzerland. I believe · God showed me at Caux that I didn't work well with those in authority over me. This was particularly clear in the wrok situation and one night I wrote out the names of bosses in various contexts and from various employments where relationships had been bad. I could get along with the staff reasonably well, but bosses were more difficult! True to the teaching of MRA I wrote letters of apology. I wrote a letter of apology to the chairman of my previous company. I wrote a letter to the Deputy Chairman whose personal assistant I.was in the company before that.

The idea in MRA was that you didn't apportion blame, and if you were *partially* to blame you apologised. 'Power that corrupts. Or power that liberates?' That was the theme of the conference at Caux. That was my theme in the message I gave to the Llandudno Liberal Assembly. At Caux I believe the human spirit dominated. The *power* of the *human spirit* was to the forefront. It was so with me. Also it was so at the Liberal Assembly. I hadn't yet come upon the *power* of the *Holy Spirit*.

As my story went on, I moved beyond MRA and deeper into Satan's territory. I still didn't recognise MRA for what it was. It is open to other religions. It reckons without the uniqueness of Jesus. It certainly isn't Christ-centred. It is a tangent to divert us away from the real thing. Perhaps it made a significant contribution in hastening my departure from church life in 1966; after all 'Remaking Men' had become my bible. But much more dramatically in 1980, on the very next day after the peace on the train, Satan zoomed in and took me off on this 'tangent'.

I had been a Christian for several months, and baptised in the Spirit, and even then I still didn't have the full assessment of Moral Re-Armament. There is plenty of room for the wiles of Satan in Moral Re-Armament. I knew very well 2 Corinthians 11: 14 NIV

Yet still I did not know the truth of Moral Re-Armament. I had for some months been born again as a Christian. I had admitted that I had sinned in the sight of God. I hated sin and was willing to turn from every thought, word, action and habit that I knew to be wrong. I believed that Jesus Christ died on the cross for me bearing the guilt and penalty of my sin. I had considered how it would be, with the opposition and misunderstanding that Jesus had, and that it would never be easy. I considered that every part of my life, work, time, friendships, money and all the rest would have to come under His control. I had asked Jesus to come into my life as my Lord and Saviour – Saviour to cleanse me of my sins and Lord to guide and be with me. I became a Christian all right. I was 'saved'. I had fellowship with Jesus in a personal way. But still I didn't understand about Moral Re-Armament.

Of course the Lord still had a great deal of tidying up to do in my life. That will always be so. In the few months after becoming a Christian I must have read close on a hundred Christian books including on Spiritual Warfare and allied subjects. I had bought 'Hidden Warfare' by David Watson in the early days. For some reason this is one book I always put on one side to read later! This was the only one with any reference to Moral Re-Armament! This is what David Watson wrote about the '*method* of the cult':*

Usually there is a simple formula or technique for "blessing". Recently, I studied carefully the Moral Re-Armament textbook titled REMAKING MEN. There is no reference in it to Christ except once where his name is quoted in the verse of a hymn. There are just four absolutes – Absolute honesty, purity, unselfishness and love. This is the secret of it all. Follow the four absolutes. In any cult the formula or the technique replaces a living relationship with Jesus Christ.

*'Hidden Warfare' by David Watson (STL Publishers)

I had been blinded by the fact that MRA seemed to set me off on the road to knowing Jesus. Even with the help of correspondence with David Watson I came only very slowly to see it is really a tangent which diverts away from the real thing only to be found in Jesus Christ. As David Watson wrote to me, 'Often the good is the enemy of the best'.

I cannot be writing this book from the standpoint of a theologian or even of an experienced Christian of many years standing. I write only as someone with a testimony to give, and including the pickings of an extensive and full-time search, sparked on that day in the train, kindled by MRA, and set on fire by the discovery of the spiritual power which I describe in the next chapter.

6

Into Spiritual Healing and the Supernatural

I had moved a step out of the materialist world with my experience on the train. I didn't have any thought of the description at the time, but I immediately became a full-time 'searcher'. In my heart I knew there was something I hadn't found. The world seemed to be starting to make sense, but it was as if there was still a section missing from the jig-saw puzzle.

One thing I very seldom did was listen to the radio, and certainly never in the middle of the day! I switched on, and just about to start was a programme about 'Healing'! It was to be the first of two, both of good duration, looking in a serious way into the claims of psychic healing. In the second programme, a couple of fairly hard-headed journalists had challenged to be shown they too could be healers as was claimed for them in the first programme. At least one of them was in good measure convinced he had a gift that could be used.

This excited me enormously. I telephoned the B.B.C. and also the Healing Centre that had been featured. I was quick to enrol for an eight-day healing course in late October. But how could I wait nearly six months! I thought, 'Isn't God wonderful? The way he sets up these things; and fancy me switching on the radio just at that time!' Things don't just 'happen'. I didn't know God. I didn't reckon Satan either. I was a long way from understanding there are two kingdoms, two spiritual dimensions and two sources of spiritual power. The one has given life, love, free will and His word; He invites you. The other is out to get you and keep you separated from God. One thing I knew absolutely nothing about was spiritual power. I was to learn fast.

Not long after the radio programme it became clear Satan wasn't going to keep me hanging around until the course in the following October. It seemed every time I picked up a local newspaper, I was reading about something in the psychic field that I could go to. My first excursion was to a demonstration of Healing and Clairvoyance. It was to be held close to my home. The venue was a very large auditorium in a spa town. You could call it the ideal setting with lots of retired people, who fit the middle-class label, living nearby. The healing demonstration was to be held in the afternoon, the clairvoyance demonstration in the evening. So there was the chance to 'take tea' between the two! There was time also to look around this little town. A few weeks earlier before the radio programme I had never heard of healing except by doctors, and a few in alternative medicine like osteopaths and chiropractors. Yet as I walked around the town I was able to collect in my diary another couple of 'Healing' engagements from advertisements displayed in shop windows. It is surprising what you see when you are alerted! It is not surprising what you miss when you are not interested! I have reflected since, how I had been blind to what was going on around me; and one of the purposes with this book is to alert to some specific and often overlooked areas of spiritual danger. One danger is to be in the cross-fire of spiritual warfare when you don't know what it's all about. That was my position then.

As I entered the auditorium I knew absolutely nothing. I am afraid that very few people knew anything at all! A very few people, Christians filled with the Holy Spirit, know a great deal. The truth is in God's word – the Bible. I didn't know that. Apart from the people on the stage that day, I remember only one person with any clarity. She was a woman. She was standing outside the main entrance carrying a big board. I don't remember what it said. Strange to reflect, I was a 'searcher' and it just didn't attract my interest at all. I just remember it said something about the Bible. It probably said something about Jesus, but I don't know. I do know it was a warning.

Inside the auditorium it soon became clear, from the conversations around, that this was some sort of big day. I had never heard of the people who were to be demonstrating to us. It was clear everybody else knew this was a 'first division' fixture! The audience was heavy with psychics and healers and they had come to see what the star performers were doing. I had never heard of the particular 'sanctuary' from which the 'healers' came. I didn't know it was famous. I didn't know its founder had been the most famous British 'healer' of all time. The healer for the day impressed me greatly and I remember particularly his story about the Roman Catholic Church. He described the procedure that had been followed prior to conferring Sainthood on a man who had brought about *one* healing. I was left with the thought that the speaker had brought about many equally spectacular healings; I had no doubt that was so. Then after the talk he went on and actually *did* it.

I was stunned by the healings this man brought about before the eyes of those hundreds of people. There was an eight year old boy made to hear for the first time. I can picture his happy face and his weeping mother on the stage. There were people that had their serious breathing problems improved. There were arthritics who hobbled on sticks and who were soon able to leap and throw their arms about them as they had never done for years. One after another the complaints were called, and the people moved up onto the stage to be healed. It seemed to me this was a great day in my life and I felt privileged to be able to witness it all. I felt a sense of pride at being in on these miracles. As I came out of the auditorium I saw the world in a new perspective. I had taken a big step, I thought. I believed I was so much wiser than those who hadn't seen these things. They probably didn't want to! I thought, 'if they haven't *seen* what I have seen, they certainly won't believe it'. I was elated. I didn't know then what I know now about spiritual powers. I had been witnessing healing by demons. Yet I hadn't come to the point of considering *why* demon spirits should want to heal anyone!

It is timely to enter a WARNING: Occult healings are not true healings. If there is not a switch from one physical illness to another, what we have is a shift of the problem from what is seen to what is unseen and the illness is shifted from the organic to the psychic, mental and spiritual areas. The latter is more serious. What happens is that an occult bondage sets in. That amounts to an inclination in the direction of occult power, with a simultaneous hardening against Jesus and the true God only to be found in Jesus. The greatest loss of all is the loss of direction towards Jesus and of the wonderful eternal life promised in heaven. The alternative to heaven – the only alternative according to the Bible – is a place in hell.

We want this WARNING to reach those who read our story whether they have experienced the spiritual dimension or not. If God has not been heard clearly, and if there is a numbness to the concept of knowing Jesus and of being born again on this earth in order to live with Him in heaven, it must be understood that the devastating effects of these occult healings are to be seen in this life on earth too. Dr Kurt Koch is a recognised authority on demonology and in his book 'Demonology Past and Present'* he writes:

'The mass of examples and observations which have been collected through the years paint a shocking picture of the spiritual devastations which result from the activity of occult healers in every branch of this disastrous profession'

*Koch, Kurt E. 'Demonology, Past and Present' Copyright © 1973 Kregel Publications, Grand Rapids, Michigan. Used by Permission.

Man is interested in overcoming illness, and so there is the opportunity for Satan and his army of demons. The other common threat to man besides illness is the uncertainty he has about death and the future. That's where mediums come in – another thoroughly dangerous area I was soon to get involved in. This was the subject of the evening demonstration in the big auditorium.

Between the afternoon and evening performances there was the opportunity to talk to people around me; I was keen to listen to those who were psychics. They told me of the tremendous power built up in the building. The conditions for healing were said to be ideal. I had one question in particular. 'There seem to be hundreds of healers here today. How common are they, and is there one that lives near me?' There was. My haemorrhoids were healed at my first meeting with her.

For the evening performance there were two clairvoyants. Both are very well-known in their field and increasingly well-known to the public generally. I did not know what a clairvoyant was until these performances, but before much time passed I was to see the same one in action again in my own front room demonstrating mediumship in the Russell Harty Show on T.V.

Tapes and video cassettes amount to a revolution in communication of spiritual material in these days. I use much Christian material in this way, but my interest started with the many tapes I listened to in those early days of discovery in the Satanic spiritual realm. The tapes greatly speeded my understanding of things from the occult side of the spiritual dimension. I was first introduced to this idea at a Healing workshop led by one internationally-known young 'healer'. I had never heard of him. I didn't know how famous he was when I saw the workshop advertised in a shop doorway, once again not far from where I live. I paid £40 for two tickets. I learned that this man was at one time well known as a spoon-bender. He was also well known for his automatic writing. Like healing, all these are supernatural abilities and my teacher had them from the time of childhood. Now he thought it right to channel the gift in the direction of healing. Like me, I am sure he wanted to help people and this was my first personal lesson in healing. So here I was, I didn't have to travel many miles for the lesson, and I didn't after all have to wait for the training course in October. I didn't know it, but this psychic healing is a growth area along with all the rest of the occult. Like witches covens, 'healing' is found all over the place in these days. You don't know where the covens are and you don't know where you will find the nearest 'healer'. Either may be located very near.

I had the warning from the lady with the board outside the auditorium. She couldn't have been more polite about it. I was getting another form of silent warning from my wife Rae by this time. The silence was to increase! By this time she had quietly registered her disapproval, or at least her hesitancy about my search. The spoon-bender's workshop, in a nice hotel in Leamington Spa, would, I thought, on any view offer a pleasant day out. I had a ticket for Rae. She didn't object, but one way or another she arranged *not* to go with me! A friend of ours, who herself had been to a 'healing' Sanctuary in the past, came in her place. I was introduced to visualisation and imagination techniques, the keys to the psychic abilities that would be developed.

It is interesting to reckon at this point that I did not by any means leave out the church view of things. I had a number of clergy friends, and other friends too who seemed active in their churches. I cannot claim I will have heard all that was said to me but I don't remember any warning. Satan is clever. He is the master of deceit and deception. He is the master of lies. There is a widespread ignorance of his wiles in these days. Apart from the two silent warnings I have mentioned, there was *one* occasion when I received a verbal warning. I am sure it was sound and articulate, but I didn't hear. It wasn't on my wavelength! The occasion was

51

one of the sessions in the main conference hall at Caux when a speaker directly behind me addressed the meeting.

The lunch followed immediately afterwards. The seating was for several hundred, and I don't believe it was man's design that brought the speaker and his wife to my table. They sat where they were put – as was the normal way with visitors. I had already found a table and was seated when someone brought them along and sat them one on each side of me. I believe the rest on the table found the couple tiresome. They went on and on. They could talk of nothing else but 'Jesus. Jesus. Jesus . . .'!

The speech that I didn't even remember was about Jesus too! I can only know what they *probably* were saying; I believe they will have been right. Their's was not a name and address that I collected. I collected dozens! I wish today that I knew their names.

I believe that couple were part of God's plan for me. I am in the same boat they were in. It will not be me that determines which hearts receive a new message from my story. The Holy Spirit is our teacher.

My direction was moving positively *against* Jesus at that time; yet He was in the situation. God's timing is different from our own. There was no natural explanation why a 'searcher' should have switched off at hearing the name of Jesus. MRA appealed to me because of its international, quasi-political multi-religious flavour; I recall actually saying, 'Jesus Christ is no big deal!' Satan is always busy in one way and another taking the opportunities that are given to him. I was opening myself up; Satan was moving in a big way now.

I shall never forget my first visit to a spiritual healer. Descriptions vary and this lady described herself as a 'Spiritual' Healer. I made an appointment to see her and I arrived full of explanation. I had, as far as I could recall, nothing wrong with me, and I reckoned this lady must be very busy indeed. 'I hope you don't mind – there's nothing wrong with me – but please can you tell me something about spiritual healing?'

I will call her Ivy. Ivy was very welcoming and she seemed happy to talk all through the afternoon. I was enthralled by her story. I heard about the spirit doctors she can see clairvoyantly and who attend to help her. Also there was a spirit of a primitive native man that helped her. She could see alongside her patient a sort of X-ray picture of the body. From her knowledge of medical diagrams she could *see* the problem where otherwise an X-ray or an operation might be necessary.

Ivy told me how she and her husband had started off as members of the Church of England. Eventually they left as I had done, and they went on to a spiritualist church. She suggested I might give it a try, and of course I did!

At the end of our long chat Ivy said 'Come on then. Let's have a look at you.' By this she meant she wanted to see if I was O.K. She placed a hard chair in the centre of the room. I sat down, and she took hold of my wrists. I thought she went into a trance, but Ivy told me this was not so. She seemed far away as she talked with her 'guides'. That was her name for the spirits, and she seemed to have an easy and personal relationship with them. She spoke to them and they communicated to her. She believed there were two spirits of deceased doctors and one of a primitive native.

At one point it rather sounded as if Ivy had been given some bad news about some unknown medical condition. She seemed very unhappy judging by the mumblings to the spirits. 'You're O.K.' she said at last. She just recommended deep breathing each day and drinking plenty of water. It was a great relief when it all ended, even though I had been perfectly fit when she started! I was most grateful for Ivy's time. There was no charge. And off I went!

But the story with Ivy wasn't over yet in the spiritual realm. In 1960 in Canada haemorrhoids (or piles) were first diagnosed. Twenty-one years is a long time and I had learned to live without thinking much about my piles. They had got worse over that long period, and particularly over the past eight years I had the daily prescription of two bran sachets in water morning and evening. It was essential I did not miss these or I risked great discomfort. If I missed twice it was a near disaster! I had an appropriately prescribed cream for that contingency. It had never crossed my mind to mention the piles to Ivy. I had learned to live with them.

Then three weeks after that session with Ivy, the penny dropped. I hadn't given my piles a single thought in those past three weeks, and I hadn't used any sachets either. My piles were gone. I had collected a box of sixty from the chemist each month, and there they were in the drawer. On a rough count there was just about three weeks' supply — forty sachets that should in theory not be there!

I was thrilled, and I called on Ivy again. We talked more and more, and the idea 'Why shouldn't *I* do it?' was taking root. I recall two other things about that visit. I remember Ivy's garden, and I thought — green fingers. This lady's garden was so perfect it seemed unreal! I was quick to conclude that the perfect fruits and flowers and the seemingly blemish-free lawn, must have been achieved with spirit help. Next, when I came to leave, a very old friend of mine was arriving. I did not know he had become disabled. He was Ivy's next patient. I was glad of another 'seal of approval' for spiritual healing. Why I wasn't just satisfied at losing my piles I don't know! I had heard of one church leader who had been treated by Ivy, and now I saw my old friend who was a senior business executive. The scene was looking more 'respectable' all the time!

There was still a long way to go before I would know Jesus. He is on the other side of the spiritual dimension and I was eventually to see some wonderful healings in *His* name. Since that day of new-found peace on the train I had never taken another tablet for sleeping, but my real healing was still ahead of me.

7

Learning to be a Healer

The conference of MRA at Caux, Switzerland had satisfied my intellect. I liked simple answers. I had seen the effect of the simple idea in private lives, and also on countries. From there moving directly on to the next venue for training as a Healer, I was into a different dimension altogether. I had tried to stimulate some interest in the spiritual dimension at Caux, but I had failed.

However there *was* a link between Caux and the supernatural. I always had a love for India. I always wanted to go to India. The three men at Caux for whom I came to have the greatest affection were all Indian. Firstly, there was a retired company director. I used to call him 'my wise man'. We had many conversations together. Then there was Rajmohan Ghandi, a well-known figure in MRA. I remembered he was well known even twenty years previously. He was the grandson of Mahatma Ghandi. I spent time with him and admired his wisdom and skill in the group. Thirdly, there was the Archbishop of Agra. He came across like a cartoon figure, big, old and crumpled, but with a fine sense of humour all the more welcome in an Archbishop. All three men impressed me and the peace they showed aroused my interest in the Eastern life.

My 'wise man' accompanied me on the flight from Switzerland and within a very few hours I was joining my new course. It couldn't have been ordered any better if Satan had seen to it personally. From the next day onwards I was practising yoga and chanting the 'OM'. My mind was still with India.

There were about thirty five members of the course and all evidently wanted, like me, to become healers. The principal teacher at the outset explained he had dowsed with his pendulum to check out the people attending. This was to make sure that we were 'right' for the course and that there would be no one to disrupt the course in any way. We all had to speak briefly about ourselves and on any view this was an interesting international group of people. There was a couple from Canada, a third-year medical student from Holland and a therapist practising Reflexology who had come from Finland. There was a Physiotherapist from the southern part of Spain. From Dublin there was an optician. There were some who were unemployed and consequently seeking to be into something new. There were the social worker-types! There were various wives who belonged to business and professional husbands! There was a jobbing plumber and one or two from a rural background. By and large this was a professional middle-class kind of group. The group was interesting for the reason that we all readily welded into it. In a strange way, all of the people did seem 'right' for the group. By the end of the week I was to be in little doubt that the selection of the group by dowsing with the pendulum ensured that the people 'intended' to be there, *were* there.

Essentially the course comprised lectures, with about a quarter of the time given over to practice. The lectures covered a wide area in the realm of the para-normal, and the whole subject was described as Extra Sensory Perception. At the outset, and by way of historical introduction, we were taken back to ancient Egypt. Training then was in the temples and you had to have an Extra Sensory Perception (ESP) in a subject to be accepted for training. Then, we were told, the system fell apart at the time of the Greek civilisation when the scientists became fed up with the temple and its 'black arts wing'.

It now seems inconceivable that any person who knew Jesus as his personal saviour and moving in His power would be attending the course. But if such Christians filled with the Holy Spirit had attended they would have assessed the nature of things at the very outset. There was recognition that paranormal gifts could be used for a variety of good and evil purposes, and the idea of a god was very clear. But without Jesus we were on a dangerous course. I didn't know Satan's plan and I felt secure there. There were, we were told, various techniques that would keep us safe from the evil aspects – the black arts wing of the present day. A pentagram was included in the techniques for our protection.

The lectures were packed with stimulating material, new facts and fresh ideas. They were deep and exciting to the human spirit. Now they are recognised as a collection of psychic, Eastern religion and pre-Christian magic. When you know of the redeeming blood of Jesus and are filled with His Spirit, you can know the truth. However this course was like a shot in the arm to an addict. Of course I didn't believe I was getting addicted. I could boast my 'experience on the train' and my new approach to life. However Satan had a plan; he was seeking to use me powerfully in his kingdom. It would still be six months before I knew the reality of Jesus.

The course showed me how 'respectable' in these days is 'healing' *without* the name of Jesus. This encouraged me because it would make it easier to share my discoveries with others. I would be able to endorse what I was doing, whenever necessary, with statements like 'You know you can get a degree in parapsychology in the USA. You know we in Britain are more advanced in this whole area than anywhere else in Europe. You know, we might be locked up in Germany for being on a course like this, but we repealed the Witchcraft Act in 1952'. And so on. The idea of 'the last days', the Bible prophecies and the Book of Revelation, were still unknown to me. I had not read how this was just as the Bible said it would be.

We were introduced to the theories and practice of many

of the therapies that have spun off from early magic and the
Eastern religions. There are so many therapies, -isms, cults,
movements, techniques; some have obscure Eastern-sound-
ing names. Others have simple innocuous descriptions.
Some are clearly to the Christian, indisputably bad. Other
practices may have an occult root, making them dangerous
apart from the practitioner himself. However care is
appropriate in approaching *any* practitioner for treatment.
In their book 'Psychic Healing – an exposé of an occult
phenomenon'*, John Weldon and Zola Levitt write the
following by way of introduction:

> 'An increasing number of practitioners in the healing profession
> (MD's, nurses, Chiropractors, etc) are being swayed by psychic
> philosophies and practises, largely due to the influence of
> parapsychology, psychic healing and the holistic health
> movements. Patients can no longer afford the luxury of failing
> to determine the spiritual status of those who treat them.'

The central figure has to be Jesus. The alternative means
opportunity for Satan. The central point of my story is that
there are two kingdoms, two spiritual dimensions and two
sources of spiritual power. The source of power in Jesus'
name is in the realm that leads to the Kingdom of God and
wonderful eternal life for those that have accepted Him as
their personal saviour. Satan has power in this world. He
counterfeits the Lord's gifts, he is a cheat and a liar, and he
can change himself into an angel of light. He can heal people
if it suits his purpose, and it is part of his plan to stop people
from knowing Jesus. He works in the spiritual dimension just
like Jesus. He is very busy in these days to keep people for his
own kingdom – a lost eternity forever separated from God.

I didn't know what was forbidden by God's word in the
book of Deuteronomy as I became increasingly proficient in
the use of a pendulum. This was perhaps the most exciting
part of the course for many of us.

*Published by Moody Press, Chicago, Illinois, U.S.A. (1982)

We saw that we had power. Of course we acknowledged it was *God's* power working through us! It hadn't seemed too difficult to persuade the two radio journalists that they could be healers. Our group hadn't been picked by the B.B.C. and it is hardly surprising that nearly everyone made good progress during the week. I was certainly no exception.

We took our pendulums outdoors too and we were able to dowse to determine the 'leylines' where the land was said to need healing. On the principle that some 'leylines' *gave* energy and some *drained* it, we were able, with our pendulums, to determine the one kind from the other and have our results checked with the existing knowledge of a skilled practitioner. We heard how lines of adverse energy flows could be corrected and that among the customers for this service were local authorities that believed they had tried every other way to obviate the dangers at accident 'black spots'. The method is to drive quartz-bearing metal rods into the ground at points determined by the pendulum. Usually the main point will be missed and we hear denials that there can be a supernatural reason for successive car accidents. Make no mistake, Satan's legions are everywhere and can take power in such places. The answer is to take authority in the name of Jesus and drive the enemy from the black spot. Deliverance and prayer are the answer. There is an upsurge in the occult but the number of true Christians where God's power flows is growing too.

It is no part of my purpose to fascinate or interest any reader – Christian or non Christian – with any aspect of the occult. Such an approach would be dangerous. Occult means 'hidden' and by God's word it should not be investigated.

In these days there is a blurring between the scientific and the spiritual. Electricity isn't understood by a good many Christians. Many just think of it as an 'energy' and they are not surprised when, in the guise of science, other 'energies' are revealed to them which they don't understand. 'Would you say electricity is occult?' I have been indignantly asked. 'Shouldn't we have prayed for more daylight hours?' As the world gets more complex, still there is *no* grey area so far as God is concerned. Electricity is scientific and can be explained scientifically. Leylines are from the father of lies in the spiritual dimension, and there is no explanation outside that context for the strange things that can occur.

This concept, which can be as damaging as a voodo figure on a mantlepiece, is yet another tool of Satan and his evil purposes are well served while men, including professing Christians, seek to resolve these questions on a scientific basis.

As regards MRA I found it is suited to Satan's purpose, for the deceived sections of the Church and the important commentators on the movement, to attack it on social rather than on spiritual ground. And as for leylines and supposed energy flows, it suits Satan's purpose to have the attention of Christians focussed on the smokescreen of false scientific analysis. Attention is thus lifted from the spiritual questions. The existence of Satan and his evil involvement is once again denied, and he has remained free to go about his business in our lives. Demons move in our church buildings too.

See how some of the arguments run! They are arguments that are futile. They are arguments to avoid. There is no use in being side-tracked. What is involved is *not* scientific. It doesn't lend itself to the worldly analysis of the archaeologists and the so-called 'ley-hunters'. It comes from Satan whose demons occupy much territory. They helped me as I searched. They can occupy objects and they can occupy buildings. They can occupy sites and 'black spots'. They can occupy churches and the land itself. I didn't then think in terms of demons, and I didn't know that, as a Christian, the Lord would later give me a practical lesson. I relate this in chapter fourteen.

What is the best analysis of the study of 'leylines' that can be presented today by a Christian? Leys are believed to be alignments between pagan temple sites; what is clear is that they do exist for the dowser today. Their pendulums or divining rods respond to them and the information is thus available. They can show where these lines cross, and unless they have become 'black spots' the energy given there will be greater; man built the temples in these places on the basis of this counterfeit faith. If you believe in the spiritual dimension, and if the belief is not of God, then it is of Satan who is glad to honour our faith, placed no matter how unknowingly, in him.

It was the early Christian custom to replace the monuments of previous religions with their own sites and churches. 'The Ley Hunter' is a magazine that deals with ancient alignments and all aspects of geomancy (a form of divination), folklore, pre-historic and ancient sites, earth energies (they say 'possible' earth energies) and strange phenomena, and in the 'Winter 1981' issue an experienced ley hunter, John Michell wrote the following:

> The occurance of churches, crosses and other later features in alignments with megalithic sites may not be much help in a statistical approach to leys, yet this pattern is just what you would expect to find given the early Christian custom of replacing the monuments of previous religions with their own.

Thus it can be imagined that much of the fun for the ley hunter is in identifying old churches, religious ruins and monuments that form straight lines across the countryside. Archaeologists are most often not interested but Professor R.J.C. Atkinson of Cardiff University made a rare contribution to 'The Ley Hunter'. He wrote that he needed to be convinced by evidence measured on the ground that such alignments were not 'chance'. So while the ley-hunter argues with the archaeologist, the experienced dowser, well established in the spiritual dimension, albeit in Satan's realm, has long since had his answer. A ley hunter writing with some spiritual sensitivity to this was Nigel Pennick

61

and he wrote, again in 'The Ley Hunter' debate (Archaeologists versus Ley hunters), as follows:

> It seems to me that archaeologists are unwilling or unable to change their mental outlook from modern scientific-materialism to that of the 'primitive' mind (for the want of a less 'loaded' word), even though we have ample record of this outlook in modern times from the holy men of Tibet, Madagascar, Australia and the Americas. The modern mind cannot conceive of a system in which the nonmaterial world takes precedence over the material, the sacred over the profane, and hence cannot comprehend that human activities can be governed by things other than economic sociological criteria.
>
> The scientific-materialist mind believes that phenomena such as divination or geomancy have no validity today, and by flawed logic, to have had no significance or even existence as belief systems in the past, hence any evidence for them is also held up to ridicule. An unconscious reverse nationalsim which can grudgingly accept geomantic practices in far-off lands as separate as China and Peru, but not in ancient Britain, seems to have its origins more in the psychological than the logical.

That very well describes a common viewpoint. Indeed it was my own. Let there be no mistake I now regard this whole area as a dangerous one that should not even be looked into, at least not outside of the guidance and protection of the Holy Spirit; but the above quotation does show an awareness of the spiritual dimension. That is where I was; I hadn't met Jesus in the Christian side of that dimension. The Holy Spirit should be sought for the answers, not the dowsers of our day or the holy men across the world in India or Tibet.

Perhaps because of religious inhibitions but more certainly because of the lack of discernment among professing Christians, and notwithstanding the clear connection of these lines with our older churches, there seems to have been very little Christian contribution to this subject. Searches into the occult are as much forbidden as the actual practice of the occult itself, so this is to a degree understandable. I have to thank God that He drew me back from my dangerous enquiry into the hidden mysteries, but that I am able to make this contribution.

Back now to the classroom on our course, we were all asked to draw plans of the houses we lived in. With our pendulums over the plans we would be able to practise, and at the same time check with the lecturer to see if we were correct. With the 'yes' and 'no' answers of the pendulum we would find out whether the energy flows were good, in which case they were called 'white'. If they were adverse, like the accident black-spots, they were called 'black'.

It was explained to the class that energy ley-lines were frequently found between the standing stones that could still be seen across the countryside. We were told that the disturbance of these stones over the years had had an adverse effect on energy flows and this had affected many of the old churches. Built on the old pagan sites where the stones and temples once stood, and with the general disturbance of the countryside including urbanisation, many white ley-lines had turned into black. The effect, we were told, was often to be found in the run-down state of the congregations in many of our churches. We were told that vehicle accidents often occurred by these black areas.

I recalled that my wife and I between us had five road accidents in the first nine months after moving to Walborough. During the lecture it seemed uncanny how so much related to Walborough.

We had lived next door to an extremely old church dating back to Saxon times. I remembered the friendly church-goers who passed by our house on the way to church. Yet I remembered the vicars who were our next door neighbours; it seemed their job was an extraordinarily onerous and difficult one. There were three different priests during our time there, and I remembered thinking I wouldn't have liked their job! Also I reflected on the time I had spent when laid up — after my *third* car accident on the nearby lanes.

All in the class drew plans and with varying success the pendulums were brought out and the answers determined. We did this in a group and so had the advantage of checking one with another; results were invariably better in the group.

I was working with *two* plans. Firstly, there was my present house. Then I thought of our time in Walborough. We could not settle the result in our group. However the teacher was an internationally-renowned practitioner in this field. It was time consuming, but he not only identified the energy flows but dowsed to get an accurate location of the lines.

First he worked on our new home, and with an amazing speed he worked through what might have been hundreds of 'yes' and 'no' answers to locate the line which ran through the building. Although I didn't doubt his reliability, professionalism or expertise in any way, I was careful not to tell any of my story or give any clues at the outset. He identified a white ley-line that passed through the office at my present house. This was where I had spent much time both at our business and in the course of the 'search' during the previous twelve months. So I was encouraged! I asked him to dowse for the church at Walborough. His conclusion was quite simple and straightforward. A black ley-line ran straight through it. Of course I didn't know I was receiving information that had been supplied by demons.

The peace that came to me on the train to London related to the time of bridging loans and changing homes. Now given the information of the ley-lines, it seemed to be confirmation that the spiritual forces were after all on my side when I made that *financially* disastrous move. This all seemed like a pretty fair analysis, but it was not until many months later when, filled with the Holy Spirit, I would understand that the ley-line information was provided by demons. It had to be disregarded according to scripture.

A burden for the village had begun soon after my

experience on the train. Prompted by Moral Re-Armament I reflected upon how much there was to enjoy in the village and how little of my time I had, particularly in the recent years, given back. The effect of this diagnosis with the pendulum was that I remembered the burden. I began to see a way to do something in return at last.

There was much in the training course that others understood and I did not. Some had become more deeply involved, were more sensitive and more aware; or they were better endowed with the psychic 'gift'. At any rate these were the explanations as I understood them. One of the ideas that I found difficult to grasp related to what was being termed 'polarity'. This polarity was said to vary and to differ from one person to another. I have no better understanding of the theories today and it is no part of my purpose to do any further research on matters where the detail would normally be of no interest to the Christian. However it is relevant to 'my story' to say that, when we moved our household electrical equipment from Walborough to the new house, one by one the items broke down beyond repair! At the time I was on the training course, I was in correspondence with the local electricity authority; I believed that the supply meter was recording backwards! When told by John, an evidently experienced student of such phenomena, that this all related to the 'polarity' that had been brought from Walborough, I was very confused! On the course we had been advised about diagrams we could draw and put on top of the T.V. set to cut down on the radiation; once again I found it difficult to assimilate! However with all that I had seen and heard I couldn't dismiss anything. Anything could happen!

I don't always *understand* when I hear of the happenings in the supernatural field. Even as a Christian *I have learned not to dismiss them.* I have, I believe, learned to draw the line at unhealthy interest. I had to become a Christian to understand the occultist view of these strange phenomena. All I could add to the facts as regards our electrical equipment was that those who were into the occult could see connections with earth energies and polarities. They were being fascinated, deceived by the father of lies.

Quite simply I didn't understand this particular area. It seemed to be no mystery to others. But in due time my 'search' was over and I grew as a Christian. I came to the point of learning that demons were out to make me fascinated by them, and I marked the famous words of C. S. Lewis in 'The Screwtape Letters':*

> There are two equal and opposite errors into which our race can fall about devils. One is to disbelieve in their existence. The other is to believe, and to feel an excessive and unhealthy interest in them.

Most of all I *now* remember the Healing Course for the friends that were made there. As I left the course my thoughts were only of the remarkable things I had seen done, that I had done, and that I would do in the future with these gifts that had been uncovered. I had said it recently, and now I was recounting it: life would never be the same again! I was now well into the spiritual dimension. I knew about spiritual power. Returning home, how would I tell it all to my wife? Already Caux and Moral Re-Armament seemed a long time past, and I last saw my family even before that. Satan was giving me a crash course all right, and he wasn't going to let the journey home be uneventful.

I arranged to travel home with a lady who was going to Manchester. I would catch the train there for Wolverhampton; Olga, who also travelled with us, would catch her flight to Amsterdam. Olga was a medical student who seemed to spend much of her time in a trance-like state. The drive to Manchester was a long one and we were just half-an-hour or so out on the quiet moorland road when I spotted something coloured by the side of the road. Road

*Published by William Collins, Sons & Co. Ltd – London

point I was making. I was 'into' the supernatural and she just didn't want to know!

Satan did eventually capture my wife's interest in his spiritual power game. That was not for another few months yet. Her interest was to last for just one day before the Lord pulled her back in a very real way. As for me, I still had some distance to travel. With all the names, addresses and ideas I had collected, both from Caux and from the Healing Centre, there was still a lot of mileage in my search. It became even more intensive.

8

Getting in Deeper

When I arrived home from the MRA conferences in Switzerland and from the Training Course there was a letter awaiting me from the church in Walborough. About this time each year the driveway to the church became untidy and overgrown. I owned the adjacent field alongside the drive and next to where we used to live. This was a letter asking me to tidy it up. It had become urgent through my long absence and the more so because there was a funeral scheduled.

My contact with Walborough had been minimal since leaving, and on the second day back I went there and set about clearing the weeds. Certainly I felt different from the time I lived there; and I shared with Jane, another neighbour of the church on the other side of the drive, what I had been up to, at least about Moral Re-Armament. My stories about the pendulum would have been just 'too much'! I didn't know it but a new relationship was beginning. Indeed it was – and it was set to progress along a course I could never have imagined.

A few days later I attended the funeral for which I had prepared the drive. My wife and I had met many good friends through the introduction of the man who had died. In particular I remembered that he had introduced Bill and his wife, Rita. They were long past retirement from a regular ministry in the Church. They never seemed to push religion at us, and they had become very good friends of ours. I had not seen Bill for well over a year, and he was conducting the funeral. We had more than a fair share of conversation in the churchyard, and once again I felt a new relationship was beginning. Indeed it was, and yet again in a way I never could have imagined.

I had an affection for Walborough that was absolutely renewed. I had a burden for the village too, from the MRA conference in Switzerland, and magnified by the pendulum diagnosis I had received. It was no part of my search. I wanted to give something back to the village. I had already planned for ley-line experts to come and treat the adverse energy flows that had been diagnosed. I regarded that as a matter of great importance but my affection and burden was more personal.

The treatment with iron rods driven deep into the ground around the church and lost beneath the surface would be a silent and anonymous operation. I could not sensibly talk to my friends in Walborough about that; but 'alive' and still with the peace discovered on the train, I was ready to meet people. I didn't know what, but I believed there was something more I had to give to Walborough.

Back from my healing and dowsing training course I now sat with various mediums. I very soon accepted it as a fact that they could give accurate information to their sitters. I shared my own experiences with others. Always it was taken for granted that communication with the dead *had* taken place. Those I spoke to who had themselves visited a medium, and got a message, were in no doubt about it. No-one warned me of the dangers as I went about sharing and up-dating the story of my search as it progressed; and no-one was able to inform me that the messages were not from the dead at all. The messages are given to the medium by demons. Let there be no doubt about that!

Thus here we have another area where growth is to be seen in these last days. I visited six mediums. The last occasion as I have related in chapter one was in a spiritualist church and in spite of my previous experience I was dumbfounded by the nature and accuracy of the information told to me. On just one occasion, a lady medium could tell me nothing. Looking back to that, the evening was exceptional and I remember I was in a researcher's frame of mind and not with her 'in spirit'. I was asking many questions. I remember that I used the word 'occult' and this dear old lady asked me please not to choose the word. Her reputation as a medium was well-established and she had been especially recommended to me, but after about four hours she despairingly announced 'I'm getting nothing.' I called the next day with a large bunch of flowers to cheer her up and thank her. All the other mediums gave accurate information.

All of the mediums I went to might fairly be described as slightly odd! But that is hardly surprising! One of them worked by reading the aura – the halo effect that she is able to see around the human body. My aura was described as very healthy. This woman saw it as green which indicated the healing gift. This was of course exactly what I wanted to hear but I was always most careful not to talk at all to the medium in advance of the sitting. I gave no clues. She explained that most people she saw in the bus-queue were so dull and boring they had hardly any aura at all. I was later to meet what I believed was the spirit of the Indian God-man Sai Baba and of him it was said that his aura was golden and reached out into the distance. I didn't realise all of these things were demonic manifestations.

Another medium could never answer the telephone when I rang him up. It is not easy to relate the experience of another but in some way it appeared he was troubled excessively by what he believed were spirit communications or vibrations. By the same reasoning he was seldom able to go shopping in a crowd without being greatly troubled by vibrations. A young man, he lived like a prisoner in his own house – and a prisoner in the worst of all ways. The vibrations are important to those in the occult. It is a demonic experience and for example most are vegetarians and believe the vibrations of vegetables, coming from the earth, are better than with animals and meat!

I spent much time in London after the first course of training. I knew London was the best place to find out about most things, and there were many things to follow up. A regular weekly visit over several months was to a basement in Highgate to visit with a man I came to describe as my London-guru. He seemed to have great wisdom and the answer to every question. If he didn't give an answer, my way was to excuse him and applaud him for being wise enough not to give it!

My London-guru was a man I listened to with great enthusiasm. He was not from India. But essentially he was a man with those secrets from the East. He knew a peace in spite of a life full of accidents and problems. He could sit for hours without being too hot or too cold, whatever the temperature around him. He never needed to fidget or move about. He had a permanent expression of peace in his face.

In company with others, I was learning visualisation and how to mentally control body functions not normally within human control. We had machines to measure our achievements. In all areas but one I was among the least successful in the group. Many of the ladies in particular were able to control their body temperatures very effectively. This was not done by 'willing' the temperature up or down but by 'visualising', 'imagining' or 'thinking' it up or down. It was possible to control heartbeat and other bodily functions. The purpose was to develop and strengthen the 'inner self'. Of course Yoga and meditation were important. I am thankful that I was not very good at that either. I was the joker in the pack and not infrequently I would be looking around at everybody else!

However the seed had long since been sown that I would be a healer. While others were wired up to the Electrical Skin Resistance machine or the Temperature Meter or the Electro Myograph or some other bio-feedback instrument, I always made a bee-line for the Electro Encepholograph apparatus. The great advantage of this sophisticated equipment was that laymen could obtain immediate and clearly understandable readings. The Electro Encephalograph (EEG) apparatus had a system of lights which showed the wave forms from both halves of the brain simultaneously.

The idea we sought to achieve with the EEG was a pattern that was described as 'State 5'. This is the particular area where I came into my own. I was usually very pleased with myself when the room lights went out and my red lights could be seen by all to be in perfect balance. As I understood it, the right brain (the intuitive side) needed to be balanced with the left brain (the calculating side). In that state, it was said that healing could take place. My mind was untroubled when in that state. More significantly, although I didn't realise it, my mind was empty affording the opportunity for something hidden and undesirable to fill it. Much to the interest of the group I would be given calculations to do and the idea was to do them without too much effect on the pattern of light. I was coming to the stage too where I could open my eyes without having too much effect on the pattern. Strobe lighting (the sort of flashing light you find in a Disco) was available, and for several months I would spend some time each day flashing this into my eyes. I had my own equipment. The use of this was linked in with the EEG machine, and it was said that this psychelitic stimulation by the light has a very powerful effect on the rhythms of the brain, affecting all parts of it. The rhythms of the two parts of the brain were said to follow this stimulation and become synchronised with each other to promote a different subjective state.

Over the period of six months in the company of my London-guru and his charming and helpful wife, an enormous range of techniques were looked at. A great deal was learned. A guru is defined as 'a Hindu spiritual teacher'. My man in London fitted that description perhaps as well as any Englishman could. The warning cannot be too often given: check out the spiritual status of whoever you are dealing with for everything genuinely spiritual must be in the name of Jesus. But that wisdom came only later. I was still into the occult ways of the East. I attended another course.

This teacher had moved on from his position as a masseur where some force was required. I was taught the method of gentle touch to correct these structural misalignments, and in the advanced lessons this led to a method where touch was not necessary at all. It was within the scope of the advanced practitioner to influence the structure of the body through what were described as the etheric reflexes of the aura. I was very aware of the spiritual power working through the leader of this course. Much was beyond my comprehension but it was no less real for that.

One of my last discoveries, before the greatest discovery of all, was Satya Sai Baba. His name had come to me from various quarters and from reading. I knew India produced God-men but this man seemed the most extraordinary. As I understood it, he put himself on a level with Jesus Christ. I was searching and had no reason to question it on the basis of what I had heard and read.

Now much used to 'coincidences', I was on the train, again from Birmingham to London. I had decided that on one of my trips I must find out about this God-man from the most reliable source. I had no idea what that would be. I was meeting a friend from the healing course to have some lunch. He chose the venue. It happened to be directly opposite the principal centre in London for information about Sai Baba, pilgrimages to his Ashram, and for the sale of everything connected with this Indian god. Remarkable coincidence or Satanic plan?

I crossed the road and was received very courteously. Arrangements were made for me to attend a little later to see the video-film made in India. This showed spectacular ceremony and magic. All was relevant to me; in view of all I had experienced there was no reason to doubt what I was seeing. There was no reason for me to doubt the story of the young man at the Centre when he told me that the wedding ring on his finger had been materialised out of the air by Sai Baba before his eyes and presented to him. Still today as a born-again Christian, I don't doubt that Sai Baba can be made to appear in materialised form on the other side of the world. I don't doubt that he can pick fruit off trees out of their season. I don't doubt that he doesn't need sleep. I have known some extraordinary phenomena near to home when the wrong spiritual forces are tapped; so I didn't doubt that India could improve on my experience. Thus when I came across Sai Baba I was very excited indeed.

Never did I meet Sai Baba in the flesh, but perhaps I did the next best thing! My time with the occult was running out, otherwise I am certain I should have gone to India. The first medium I had seen had me clearly in line for distant travel in that year, as well as success in healing. I had made the travel enquiries and it was there written on my pad: 'Gulf Air Return London-Bombay-London £310; Bombay-Bangalore internal £95'.

I came away from the Sai Baba Centre with an address in London I was recommended to visit; if I went there I would see sacred ash manifesting. I was told Sai Baba went there most days, and that that house happened to be the place where Sai Baba was most active at that time. I left the Centre with some of this ash (called vibhuti). There was no charge and I was told that a pinch of it mixed in lukewarm water, if taken orally, morning and evening, 'with faith and sincere prayer' to Sai Baba (or to my own chosen God), would be expected to relieve any distress whether emotional, physical or mental. They said that God was so kind that he always listened to his devotees' sincere prayer and the only thing I had to do was to have faith in him and 'surrender'. I wasn't too far off from having that faith; and I did pray to Sai Baba on one or two occasions.

The modest address in the East End of London was oc-cupied by a delightful couple from the East; and the lady of the house, Indian in appearance, actually came from Indonesia. They had never seen Sai Baba in the flesh and had never been to India.

Once again there was no question of my disbelieving the main elements of what I was told. I accepted then what these people told me; as to their experiences I don't doubt them even today. After the welcome, I was asked to remove my shoes and we went to the puja or prayer room. One of the bedrooms had been turned into the prayer room and the children were having to double up. The lady used to have a statue of Sai Baba beside her bed and it was at that time that the sacred ash began to appear on the statue. As fast as she would remove it, then overnight it would reappear. Interest spread around and visitors brought their statues and photographs for blessing, including some of Jesus Christ. More and more visitors came and it was necessary to set aside a separate room. My hosts spoke of the professors, experts and authorities of various kinds that had visited, and this had been going on for two years. There was a distinctive aroma in the room left by Sai Baba when he called. Others came to see what it was all about while I was there. I sat cross-legged for three hours but I was never made to feel other than very welcome, and all of my questions were dealt with by these humble people to my great satisfaction.

The position of my hosts was that they were very honoured to play their part for Sai Baba. They were, they believed, on a very low rung of the ladder, and they said that clearly their faith was so bad that Sai Baba had to keep showing them this ash. They believed that there were many in London and throughout the world who were praying to Sai Baba in faith and who had never needed any such manifestation.

It was clear they would accept no contribution or money for whatever reason it might be offered. They were delightful hosts and I remember them with a lasting affection. After I was born again I sent them a copy of 'The

79

Gentle Breeze of Jesus', the story of miracles and the Timor revival. This little book, given to me by Jack Mowate, my clergyman friend, couldn't have been anything but an excellent choice for me as I pursued my course in the wrong direction. I pray that it may yet speak to my friends in that small London home. There was something different about my friends. They were simple hard-working immigrant people showing no sign of ego. As far as I know they had no gifts given to themselves and there was no reward save the knowledge that they did the will of their god, that they were working out their karma and probably expecting a better position in a later reincarnation.

After the visit I needed to cross London to spend the evening with my London-guru; as ever his wife was there too. I was excited as I boarded the Southern Region train to Stratford East. There I stepped out to cross to the Underground train a few yards away. And wow! Sai Baba's aroma flooded all around me. There was no mistaking it – that powerful smell once again. It came, and quickly it left. I boarded the other train. Now for the doubts. But no, there was no way I could get any smell from my clothes, even by burying my nose in my coat. The tale I would tell to my guru had got even better since leaving my new friends. This was to be the last evening of my training course in Highgate.

My London-guru had done a good deal of work with another Indian God-man. He had told many tales about how he could move at will the needles and lights on the bio-feedback machines. I hadn't taken the same interest in this god-man that I had taken in Sai Baba because I believed in the superiority of Sai Baba. I had heard that when other gods met him they fell at his feet.

I was told a story of what occurred after this other god-man had left following a visit to that Highgate basement. My guru's wife got the strong smell of the Swami's perfume and a vision of him in a red robe. She said she had a very clear vision of him in that robe. He wasn't wearing a robe as he sat wired up to the bio-feedback gear and the lady never saw him in such a robe in the flesh in London! Until the station at Stratford East I had never heard of perfumes being flushed in that way, and now I was getting the idea confirmed from the guru's wife. The lady was able to match my experience! Shortly after the aroma and the vision, she had received a gift photograph from the Swami; on it he was wearing the red robe. The devil was so often there ready to confirm and reassure. I didn't then know this was a carefully contrived counterfeit of how the Lord gives confirmations to *His* children.

9

Lifeline to Jesus

We cannot know the Lord's wisdom or rationalise His way of working out His plan in our lives, but Jesus drew me to Him by way of my experience and friendship with a friend in the occult named John. My Anglican clergy friends were significant too. One of them, Jack Mowate, had taught me in the course of my search that the clergy cannot bring people to Jesus but can only be available. This availability together with the care of other friends was to be a blessing. But John was the one the Lord would use for the great turn around to Jesus.

As I sailed excitedly through the realms of the occult I liked to hold on to my church background as something of an insurance policy. That is what it turned out to be. From the start of my search I scarcely made a move without reporting afterwards to one of my friends. One was a local farmer and we spent an evening each week through the winter gently getting to the bottom of what seemed to be my problems, rebuilding my moral character (along MRA lines) through sharing them and eventually making a start on the Bible itself.

Also I was to remake the acquaintance of Jack Mowate, who was a curate at one of the large churches in the centre of the town – perhaps the first church I ever remember attending, as a five year old for an Ascension Day service with my Primary School in 1943. We trusted their reliability and their Christmas card was the one we knew would not fail to come. They were as remote for the rest of the time as the most distant of our friends.

Just about the time I started my interest in spiritual healing I learned that Jack was in the Intensive Care Unit at the local hospital after suffering a heart attack. When I heard that, the flash to my mind was: 'I hope he gets better because he will help me.' I had no problems that I could see; I just believed he was going to help me, and I believed that most strongly. I felt also a sadness that after a relationship of sixteen years, I hardly knew him. 'Yes, he must get well,' I thought to myself.

After a few weeks I learned that Jack was home from hospital and I planned to visit him. But before that I met Jack face-to-face in a bookshop. I was browsing on what I now know as the 'occult' shelf. Of course the book stores don't usually recognise it as such and any Christian books are often mixed in with the spiritual and the psychic! I was looking through a copy of 'You Live after Death' that I had been recommended to buy. I turned around and there was Jack. After all of the pleasantries and good wishes, I couldn't wait to ask, 'What d'you think of this?' It might have been any book in this new area of my interest, and my question would have been the same. Not surprisingly he had never read this particular book, and so he couldn't answer. I mentioned my new approach to life that had started on the train.

I had never heard of Divine Healing, and Spiritual Healing was something that was to me an entirely new and recent discovery. 'I have had a healing ministry for four years,' Jack told me. You could have knocked me down with a feather! We moved away to a coffee shop, and I hope I didn't overtax his strength! When he was leaving with the promise of books for me to read, I said, 'I'll have the books right away; I might have moved on to stamp-collecting if we delay!' I knew in my heart this was not true. I was on to something big, although I didn't know what. Jack knew it too. 'You'll never get away now the Lord has put His finger on you,' he said.

Jack told me he had been walking with his wife in Burnham-on-Sea when he saw a book in the window of a store that caught his attention: 'Your Healing is within You', by

Canon Jim Glennon. Jack bought the book, and he said he simply did what the book said. Parishioners go to him for healing. He lays his hands in Jesus' name and they are frequently healed. It became clear that Jack had successes no less significant even if sometimes less spectacular than those I had seen at Spiritualist Healing demonstrations. Of course they were *more* significant, because they were in Jesus' name.

It seemed then that I had a sort of endorsement for what I was doing. Jack never gave his OK to what I was up to; it was rather that I was delighted to know that there was a 'respectable' Anglican also doing some healing! I didn't know the difference between his sort and my sort. Nobody had in any very significant way objected to what I was doing. I had an idea that not all would approve, and it seemed I had a sort of implied approval from the church in which I had been brought up.

It is true that Jack's ministry served me well. However I talked on this subject with a good number of clergy friends and acquaintances, as well as others from the ranks of intelligent and Christian lay-people, and never was I *aware* of words of caution. The Lord's timing would be perfect.

As I had learned of Jack's plight in the hospital, I knew he was the man to help. And now I thought I could see how that would be; Jack was a Healer himself. But that was not the reason. I believe Jack's word that the Lord had a finger on me was from the Lord Himself. However the real need for Jack's ministry had not yet come. The Lord's alarm bell was yet to ring. It would be loud indeed; and still Jack would be there.

The path was marked out through my time on the training course. It was not until the end of the time of training that I met John. It was not until the end of those days in the group together that he manifested his extraordinary 'healing' capability. He seemed like the shining star of the group and I was introduced to him by another friend, herself very capable, as the one with the best understanding of the forces at work to make healers. Our group leader had said that it was all ESP. Now after the official sessions were over I was meeting John for the first time. Like me he was no more than a searcher who was there to learn, but I was learning from him about spiritual planes, reincarnation, and many bits and pieces that fitted very nicely into my jig-saw. John was an articulate educated widower. To add to these credentials, and that is how I saw them, he had himself been 'healed' by one of the best known spiritual healers. His own 'healing' was so extraordinary it had been featured in his best-selling book.

There was no difficulty in keeping touch with John after we went our separate ways at the end of the course. That is the way it was, and there were many telephone conversations about our own 'progress' and that of our mutual friends in the group. We were all part of what seemed a close-knit club and there was a good understanding between us. We had all done 'powerful' things together; we knew an awareness that others did not. We were different! There were many letters exchanged, and hundreds of miles were travelled as we kept in touch with one another. I learned from John that he was to be a Healer like the man who had healed him and he wrote of the 'same terrific healing force' that he would have. There was no way for me to recognise the slippery slope he was on. He informed me that he would be used to combat arthritis and rheumatism in particular, but 'almost everything else' as well. Nothing in all this struck me in the least strange and he wrote that he would meet another healer who would attend to the admin side involved in his healing work. He said it would be a man with whom he had had many 'close lifetimes' and they would travel the world for about twelve years. When he told me of the trials, bad experiences and 'tests' he had had that 'weren't at all funny' no alarm bells rang. Why a searcher, travelling at the pace I was moving, didn't question, I am only now as a Christian in any position at all to judge. Satan was my Search Director!

John was thrilled at the prospect of progress beyond the pendulum. 'Thank God, because it takes time getting a lot of information by "yes" and "no" answers,' he wrote to me. He was becoming clairaudient, his 'guide' Michael had told him. As he told more of his story it was more than my mind could understand – but I remained in a sense open-minded. He wrote with lists of books and in his letter he said 'They are TRUE, UNQUESTIONABLY'. Always in my life I had been one to question everything that interested me; but it did not occur to me that he needed help. I think Satan was my Course Tutor as well as Search Director!

Within a month John was diagnosed to have cancer, and he told me his GP had given him six months to live. He was in the highest possible spirits as he gave this news to me, and as I joined with him I had not the least gloom on his behalf. His enthusiasm for the idea that he would be healed by Christmas, just as his 'spirit guide' had told him, was totally infectious and we talked about the usual subjects as was our way. In the months following I know that John suffered but he bore it very bravely saying it was all to 'test' him. I never knew him except in the highest of spirits. He was being deceived. I was being deceived.

It was clear from what he was telling me that, without medical treatment, his cancer was abating. He told stories of the amazement of his GP as he measured the declining size of his lumps. Next came his torment. I was telephoned to say that John was under attack from evil spirits. A friend rang to say that he seemed to be under constant threat from them and was to be found running around the bedroom to escape them. I had never heard of the 'anti-christ' but John apparently saw this as the problem. He arranged crucifixes around the bed and pictures of Jesus were brought in from all around; John, an Anglican churchgoer, was himself seeking to exorcise the evil spirits in this futile way. John was seventy miles from me, and I was learning of this torment from a close and mutual friend. Even so there was no ringing of alarm bells. I was asked to pray, and I did, but I felt sure John could handle the situation and come through.

In a couple of days I received a telephone call. I had been trying to contact John. He was dead. I did not discover the reason for death. I presumed it was the cancer after all. Certainly I hadn't heard the full story at that stage.

Events were now to move very fast in my life; I would soon *know* the Lord Jesus. For the past five Sundays I had been to church. As far as I was concerned this was an intellectual decision; my search had moved into a new phase. I was 'into' the churches! After all I had better see what is going on in the churches! I had in mind to mention 'healing' in these places and see what reaction I got! I had done the rounds of the local churches going to each one once according to some sort of plan.

I suppose it was inevitable I would next go to a Spiritualist Church after John had died. It was there I received the most remarkable information, the clever description of a book I had been reading called 'The Life of Jesus Christ'. What a smart choice of book to describe me! I had already come to believe in reincarnation, the idea that the dead are still alive had been 'proved' to me before, and now Jesus was conjured up. The medium introduced information that was to convince my wife – at last – that there was something in all this. Yet happily that interest, and indeed my own, was now to be short lived. We were to learn *how* John had spent his last days tormented by demons. These caused him to inflict cuts and bruises upon himself. As a fellow-searcher along with John, my future looked precarious indeed. But now, with equal enthusiasm and with a fear in my heart, I put myself wholeheartedly into the business of investigating the dangers of what I was into.

10

New Age to New Birth

I conducted a thorough investigation after John's death. It is important to state that some names, and occasionally details, have been changed throughout this book. It is my story – how things affected me – from the touch on the train and through the battle for *my* salvation. It was the effect on me of all this and of what followed that was pertinent to my story. At last I would ask the question, 'What are the dangers in all these things I have been doing?' I was to learn about spiritual warfare.

At Christmas time, just six weeks before, I had resolved to ease up on the search and make my way into more activity on the business scene. Also I was looking at the idea for the future of operating a Healing Centre, in a building adjacent to my home that had a white ley-line running through it. It was now clear there would be none of this. The big question now was: 'What are the dangers?' I *wanted* to find the answer. With a sense of self-protection, I *needed* to find the answer.

I was soon off to see Jack Mowate once again, and I asked him to lay hands on me and pray for my protection. Jack did this, and then he presented me with a wooden cross. He said he had had it for many years awaiting that moment. The cross is made of olive wood in Bethlehem, and it came with a card:

'In this sign conquer.
The Cross, which is the symbol of self-sacrifice, and death, is also the symbol of LIFE.

The Cross is the supreme expression of the Love of God and of the teaching of Christ.
The Cross is the way of life which leads to resurrection.'

I had felt vulnerable, on the run from the spiritual world that I had discovered. My mind went back to the time I heard Jack Mowate was in hospital and perhaps at death's door. 'Jack Mowate is going to help me,' I had thought then. Next to the time when I discovered the Anglican church had a hand in healing, and that Jack actually *had* a ministry. That was it, I couldn't believe it! However it wasn't to be that at all. NOW I was saying 'Help!'

Jack's ministry hadn't ended yet. I didn't know what was 'baptism in the Holy Spirit'; and he didn't tell me! He knew where I would get it; and when he saw me next I was to get my directions.

I felt by no means threatened as I believe would have been the case if I had not had my foot in the door of my various clergy friends. Not only could I run to them and say 'now hear this!', but I also felt a sense of security – false I am sure – from the fact that I had told them more or less all that I had been up to. I was not panic-stricken although in the circumstances I might have been! I certainly became more cautious. I was used to finding answers to problems. Here was an urgent one. Also I was concerned for the well-being of fellow searchers, particularly for those who I believed had made more 'progress' than me.

I had many questions about the dangers. Now I was asking. I was getting answers – a lot of answers. Back to Jack, with an enormous well-prepared list; it must have been daunting indeed! I was learning the answers to many questions on the dangers, but they were still *my* questions, and still there were many areas I was not questioning despite their danger.

One of the areas was Sai Baba. I was still very interested in what this Indian Avatar or God-man could offer me. Only in the recent weeks after going to the shrine in London had I asked my 'London-guru', a man of few words, what were the dangers. He had put his forefinger to his brow and smiled. He had one of those assuring expressions that make up for lack of words as if to say 'You wouldn't understand my answer at your present level of awareness.' However I was starting to want words as well, and when I forced him on he said something like: 'Others may have problems but you will not.' That was enough for me *then*, but by this time it was not. I was being cautious about the things I was close to. But still I couldn't get Sai Baba out of my head.

Sai Baba still had a great attraction. He was, after all, a counterfeit of Jesus. He was alive in the flesh and perhaps I had read and seen more of him than I had of Jesus. He without doubt had extraordinary supernatural powers that had, it seemed, benefitted many. I recalled the *one* problem that I had had with Sai Baba. *He* didn't approve of this so-called psychic or spiritual healing. He didn't disapprove of Jesus; on the contrary he allowed statues and pictures of Jesus to be blessed at the shrine I had been to. I could see now that healing was bad. John had been opened up to the powers of evil years ago when he was 'healed' himself. He was dead, and that seemed to prove that! Satan was still hanging on to me, and the one difficulty I had with Sai Baba was now removed. I had got to the position where I saw 'Spiritual Healing' was evil; however divine healing *through* Jack Mowate and *by* Sai Baba, who after all was alive, both seemed to be good.

I had read of an interview with Sai Baba which *previously* caused me difficulty. Now that I saw spiritual healing and psychic healing as bad, I was *totally* reconciled to Sai Baba's position. I had read up a great deal on Sai Baba apart from seeing him on film and meeting his devotees, and the *only* problem I had with Sai Baba was his disapproval of healers. I had sought to become a healer but now, as I surveyed the dangers after John's death, all that was changed. The interview with Sai Baba *at last* made sense.

That interview dialogue ran on these lines: A distinguished devotee of Sai Baba was telling him of a situation where a

Healer wished to join a Sai Baba Centre and use his healing powers for the benefit of Sai Baba's devotees. He told Sai Baba that the leader of that particular centre had had relief from illness by means of the power flowing from the hands of the Healer. He said that the leader had the idea that the Healer had been sent by Sai Baba and that Sai Baba was doing the healng through the person of the Healer, and the interviewer was asking Sai Baba for his viewpoint on this.

Sai Baba informed the questioner that the power flowing from the Healer was not his power. He said it was evil power and that the Healer himself was in need of healing. Of course Sai Baba was exactly right! Sai Baba pointed to two people who were strong and healthy suggesting that their health was due to divine power without the agency of an outside healer. That made sense also!

However the interviewer pursued the matter with Sai Baba and told him the Healer had asked him to ask Sai Baba if what he was doing was alright. The answer was that it was not, and that it was not divine power flowing through the Healer. Once again that was difficult to fault! How then should one be healed was the next question Sai Baba was asked, and once again his reply seemed entirely credible. He said the way was by prayer and by ordinary medical means.

Still undaunted, the interviewer pursued his questions with this 'god incarnate' and pointed out that there were thousands of cases around the world of sick people being healed by Healers. I could testify to that. 'What about them?' he asked. Again his answer was a close counterfeit of the Christian's position and he pointed out that any benefit is only a temporary feeling of relief and not real.

Sai Baba went on to say that if a healing occurs it is because the person has had a 'feeling or thought of God'. Still not into the Kingdom of God I was in no position to see the error in *that* statement. From where I stood it seemed clearer than ever that Sai Baba was god incarnate, and I sought Jack Mowate's advice on Sai Baba from the point of view of Sai Baba's attitude to Healers.

During this visit Jack had a word from the Holy Ghost to pass to me. As if to ensure that I took it seriously, Jack had written it out on a piece of paper which he handed to me when I arrived:

Roy—have a chat with the Rev. Michael Reynolds. He is the minister of the Elim Pentecostal Church which specialises in Divine Healing—Jack.

As he handed it to me he said: 'You can take that as having come from the Holy Ghost.' This was to bring me very close to safe ground. I would be splashing around just a little longer. There were a few more things the Lord would allow Satan to show me. Coincidences as I called them never ceased to be at work and as I look back at many of them, the results were complex and subtle. The Lord's plan or Satan's? What about this next example?

I was feeling weary through my efforts looking into the dangers and became attracted by the idea of a week or weekend away, and I had in mind the sort of retreat my vicar used to attend years ago. I suppose I had clergy on the brain! At one time I would go for a year and never *see* a clergyman! Now they seemed to be in my path all the time! Just after beginning my search into the dangers I met a priest at an Amnesty International luncheon party whose reaction was to laugh when I brought evil spirits and exorcism into the conversation. I was feeling particularly frustrated at the ignorance of spiritual power that I was now identifying. Now as a Christian, sad to say I must accept that as the simple fact. At that time I needed to get away, and at an Anglican church the following Sunday, there it was advertised in the magazine: a Retreat for lay-people. I managed a late booking and there was not long to wait. I didn't study the information, I just booked!

When I arrived I found that a central theme was meditation, which I was trying to give up! It was certainly a restful weekend as there was 'no talking', and I was afforded plenty of opportunity to revise something else I had been trying to give up! Immediately on arrival my eyes alighted on advertising posters directing to sources that only in the previous week I had come to understand as occult.

During the course of my stay there I was able to purchase for 35p what seemed to be the best guide book to occult and psychic therapies, courses, conferences, workshops, etc. that I had ever seen! I remember thinking my 22 months tour with Satan would have been so much more efficient given this practical guide book at the outset! Yet here I was at a retreat advertised in the Diocesan Newsletter including Anglican clergy and being run by an Anglican vicar. I was meditating again! I was reading about the occult again! God or Satan? I was not a little confused! I had not by that time learned what a breadth of ideas is accommodated in the Anglican Church. What I *had* already learned about was the lack of awareness in the Anglican church of the spiritual dimension. I was quite clear that many clergy, and almost certainly the majority, were unaware of the extent of the power of the Devil beyond the more acceptable idea of 'good and evil'. Still not a Christian myself, I did not know that the unawareness extended across the spiritual dimension. I had yet to learn that very many nominal Christians, including clergy, didn't know the power there was in the name of Jesus. As yet I didn't know *that* myself!

In distinction to the new, up-to-date and gloomy picture of the Church of England I was building after my time away from it, I met individual Anglican Christians who helped me greatly. The clergyman who was leading the meditations and the retreat was no exception. I remember his personal words to me. 'The searching is OK, so long as you are anchored in Christ. The Lord's timing is better than our own.'

I was helped when I shared with the leader of the retreat my burden for my old village of Walborough, based in particular upon the diagnosis for the church there. With John's death I had not surprisingly developed an antipathy for the areas with which John and I had been most active; but I could not forget the diagnosis for the Church at Walborough.

By this time I was cautious about dangers and I didn't use my pendulum any more. However I didn't doubt the accuracy. I reasoned that if you employed a water diviner and he said, 'There is water *here*,' then you would dig if you want the water. If you didn't dig then the water certainly wouldn't go away! However I was still deceived and it seemed to me that the land with the church in Walborough was draining energy; there was a presence there that needed to be dealt with. The retreat leader helped me with his comments. He said he had prayed for deliverance at accident black-spots and similar problem places, and he shared how the Lord's way, if taken, was so much better. It had, he said, been thoroughly effective.

Slowly but surely I was identifying the Lord's ways against Satan's counterfeits. I thought I might be wrong but I was still blinded by the pendulum *diagnosis* I had for Walborough. The question of 'what *treatment*?' would have to go in the 'pending' file. I had made the arrangements for the treatment on my own land adjacent to the church by sinking quartz-bearing iron rods into the ground to alter the energy flows. That was the principle more commonly applied to acupuncture of the body. On my return from the retreat I resolved to cancel my arrangements for this so-called acupuncture-of-the-earth.

The day before I took Jack's advice and went to see the Pentecostal pastor, Mick Reynolds, I had been to yet another church. Unconsciously I must have had a sort of shopping list of Churches because this was another different one, and I still hadn't attended the Elim Church. This time it was the Baptist Church at Fulbury, a small village next to the village of Walborough. For a year or so our young daughter Sue had been a member of this Church. It was a relatively lively one and in particular it had catered well for the youth mainly from the bigger village of Walborough where we lived. Previously I paid little attention to Sue's connection with the Church. She had been collected each week by the youth leader to go to Fulbury. All the people seemed very nice, and that was that! The Lord's plan had been at work long before I knew of such a thing, and assuredly it was working itself out as I attended my first service at Fulbury Baptist Chapel just one day before I was due to meet Mick Reynolds for the first time.

Kidderminster Elim Pentecostal Church was actually mentioned in that service. This gave Elim that 'seal of approval' that I again wanted. My friend, Jack, had said go there but I had passed the church many times over the previous twenty-five years that it stood there and it had seemed a funny sort of place. In fact it is a perfectly sensible and simple oblong building, neat and tidy, modern, and although in the centre of the town it even had a car park. But it had that name – Elim! What on earth did the name mean?* (See footnote)

I suppose it was not according to my experience much like a church; but how could it be that I saw it as a funny sort of place? I had never met anybody that attended there and I had certainly never seen or heard of the arm-waving and dancing during the services nor of the deliverance that took place there.

It was on February 22nd that I saw Mick Reynolds in accord with the word from the Holy Spirit that Jack had given me. Like Jack Mowate, and the leader of the retreat, his message was to get the anchor in Jesus. However he was more emphatic and positive on the question of the search. 'End your search now,' he told me, 'you are into something that is very dangerous; you are at a dangerous crossroads.' I was left in no doubt and there was no way I was going to ignore his warnings. What I recall of our long meeting is that his stories were entirely *credible* to me. They would

*When Moses led Israel from the Red Sea they came to a place 'where there were springs and seventy palm trees, and they camped near the water' and that, in the book of Exodus (15:27), was called Elim.

be *incredible* to the majority of people and it is unlikely he would have shared them with anyone totally unfamiliar with one side or another of the spiritual and supernatural dimension. He knew the path I had taken. Jack had introduced me to 'Gentle Breeze of Jesus' by Mel and Nona Tari. This Christian paperback described both the workings of Satan and the Bible-style miracles in Jesus' name in Timor, Indonesia. Added to my own experience in the occult there was little likelihood my mind would be unduly stretched by the Pentecostal pastor's extraordinary Christian testimonies.

Mick Reynolds told me of life as it really is in my own home town. He described aspects of cases in his own experience. He described deliverance sessions that had taken place in the room in which we were sitting. He described the witchcraft that he had met and a young witch who could levitate from the ground and through her bedroom window. Mick Reynolds was used in deliverance. In other words he actually got rid of demons with authority in the name of Jesus. He was the Pastor of the Elim Church. It was a Christian Church. Still I was not a Christian. I didn't know the significance or meaning of any of these labels.

I believe the Lord was using this period after John's death to allow light to dawn and to lay a few keystones for the future. I didn't realise that at that time a link was being forged between my teenage daughter's Baptist Church at Fulbury and the Elim Church in Kidderminster. When I was there the visiting preacher from Elim, Kidderminster to Fulbury was announced. As I shared about the Walborough/Fulbury connection with Mick Reynolds at our first meeting, my expression will have suggested 'What a coincidence!' However I supposed it was God's plan. Apart from the Holy Spirit going ahead of me with my daughter, I could have had no possible clue how the plan would focus on my new burden for Walborough.

For the present my interests still went into various areas

and not the least of these was my enquiry into the matter of exactly what caused John to die. My enquiry, although good-tempered, was spurred on by indignation. Not only had the police ripped out the wires to stop phone calls to the house, but next I heard that there would not even be a post-mortem or inquest and John was on the point of being buried. I had to be sensitive to his sister who I assumed would find the whole subject of demons a foreign one; but I was concerned that lessons should be learned from John's death if there were any. Surely there were, and my heart went out to my fellow searchers who it seemed would be blessed by the truth of the story, preferably from an authoritative source, if it could be obtained.

The last date I have in my diary, two days before I received Jesus into my life on my first visit to a service at Elim reads 'Bishop'. I had written to John's rector, sending a copy to the bishop. I went to see the bishop with the stated purpose of getting John's house exorcised. I understood that poltergeist activity might have been present or at least stirred up by the goings-on. That was a view endorsed by various clergy when I checked it out with them; in addition I saw it as a peg on which to hang my enquiries. This bishop had been deputed by his diocesan bishop and I presumed he was the man most able to deal with this unusual question. This was surely the opportunity to learn a great deal!

Reviewing my notes for the meeting with the bishop it is clear that I might have presented a confused picture of myself. I was giving him a problem that had to take precedence over any idea of counselling me! However I learned little or nothing from that visit whether looking at the practical and real questions involving John or looking at the theology of what was involved.

I was getting to know more about the Anglican Church and how different those in it are one from another. I was beginning already to see that there is no easy way to tie down what the Church thinks even when you talk to a bishop!

The bishop said he would pray for John and for guidance on what he should do. I left holding the view that he wasn't really 'into' the world of the supernatural such as I was describing. I was disappointed but, as was so often happening, the Lord's purpose in the meeting was perhaps different from the one both the bishop and I were intending. For me I had had my first long conversation with an Anglican bishop!

I had made ten careful notes in advance of the meeting with him and note number ten in all its naïveté summed up where I had got to just two days before being born again:

> 10. I think God wants me to be filled with the Holy Spirit. And for the beginning I think God wants me to do some healing with His Holy Spirit. Will the Bishop give me the Lord's blessing in the way that is right?'

By then I had read about being filled with the Holy Spirit (I didn't know what it meant) and I had seen Bishops bless people (this bishop wouldn't pray for me!), but what I really wanted was to be used for healing. In His wisdom God had, I believe, used the past month to lay some keystones. He thus used my enquiry into the dangers of the occult, just as he would later use my search into the occult itself.

I cannot know how any of the Lord's moves will work out in His overall plan. I would learn 'the Lord's timing is better than our own'. The keystones of the plan had been laid while I had been concerned about healing and concerned about sharing the dangers with my friends. I didn't know it, but on Sunday I would become a Christian.

I had said my search was over but not until Sunday, 7th March was it truly over. Yet another different church; this time it was the Elim Church in Kidderminster. I arrived for the evening service, warmly greeted with handshakes and books. The room was quite crowded with more than a hundred people. The Pastor I had already met took the service but the preacher for the evening was George Miller, the black Jamaican-born evangelist who had conducted the

10-day Town Hall crusade I had attended in the previous December. The day in December had made little impression; but this evening in March would be quite different.

Inside the church I spotted one face I knew. It was George Cox. George was the only member of the church I even recognised. Until his retirement after 40 years George used to clean telephones. I recalled the hundreds of times George must have come into my office to clean my telephone. I knew George to be a Christian; I don't believe I'd known very many!

I don't remember much of the service. The freedom shown in the arm-waving and the dancing was strange, but I was used to the strange by this time! George Miller invited people to go forward in the service; whether for Salvation, for Holy Spirit Baptism, for Healing, or whatever, I don't recall. I stayed in my seat. Again I don't remember why, but I had no doubt my time would come. Perhaps I thought there was some other 'right' time! I *had* gone forward at George's meeting in the Town Hall. That had meant nothing to me.

When the service was over it seemed that George left the stage and aimed himself at me where I was at the back of the hall. Our conversation led to his invitation to talk in a side room. I informed him that I wished to ask Jesus Christ into my life, that I wanted to be baptised by the Holy Spirit and to speak in tongues! I didn't really understand these things but I had been reading charismatic Christian books. Once again I have little memory of what transpired except that I prayed for these things. I didn't then speak in tongues but was assured that I could rely upon Jesus' promises that I now did have Jesus in my life and I had indeed been baptised by His Holy Spirit. My life started to change that day.

That day was the start of a *real* peace in my life – that peace which passes all understanding, and not that peace which the world seeks to give. That day was the start of a new love for people – a genuine love for every kind of person. After that day, the Bible, such a dull book for so many years without having the Holy Spirit to quicken the meaning of scriptures to me, came alive. It was clearly the truth – the truth that sets men free. After that day too, my desire was to fellowship more and more with God's people.

I was no longer a New Ager. I had experienced the New Birth.

11

A New View of the Village

I had not been a Christian for very long before I could perceive, even among those Christians who understood the occult from a scriptural point of view and from counselling others, much of my story seemed to be unfamiliar ground in the Body of Christ. Very soon, from within the fellowship I had joined, I was being encouraged to write. Little did I realise that in a matter of a few months I would have more material from my short time as a Christian than had been gathered in my time in the occult.

Clearly something needed to be written about the dangers of alternative medicine and holistic healing, but once again, before many weeks passed my heart was reaching out again to the village of Walborough. The sentiment for Walborough, birthed during my rediscovery of Moral Re-Armament, had been strong when the so-called 'blackness' was diagnosed by the diviner. The burden for Walborough, there during my excursion through the occult, had not left me. Indeed it had become stronger since the vicar I had met whilst searching the dangers told me of his prayerful methods at black spots. Now I was a Christian myself—what should I do about it? That is not to say I saw the answer was with me personally, but it did seem I had been put in a situation by God's grace and given some sort of job to do. I didn't know what! In 'Spiritual Healing' I had said that if others could do it, why not me? Now I said, if clergymen can do things in the power of Jesus, and in Jesus' name, why not me? As a Christian I was soon hearing the expression 'wait upon the Lord'. Apart from doing just that, I didn't really know what to do. Except keep praying!

Walborough is a friendly village community situated on the eastern slopes of high bleak hills close to the Welsh border. It is attractive, still relatively self-contained and self-sufficient, and well off the main road. The Norman church is in the centre of the village. My family and I moved into a house next to the church in 1971. It was a big house and after various alterations inside and to the grounds bordering the church, it was close to our idea of a 'dream house' in a perfect English village. Although born and brought up in Kidderminster, I had never even heard of Walborough, and here it was within easy commuting distance and tucked away in such idyllic surroundings. Thus I had a magnificent house, lovely family, good friends, and was well established with the leading company in Kidderminster. The national economy was booming. I was certainly prospering. Indeed everything in the garden was lovely. Yet my time in Walborough was really something of a disaster.

We lived just one hundred yards from the church. I resisted any idea of getting closely involved in its life. For the previous five years since 1966 we hadn't been church-goers. I still remembered the tiresome Parochial Church Council (PCC) meetings and all the rest that I had known up to 1966. We had reasoned after that that the new church was too many miles from our home, and the children were at the nappy stage! But really it didn't mean much to me anyway!

Looking back to where I had been, I was a regular Sunday School attender in the local Anglican church. I was baptised and confirmed, and as a teenager I became a regular churchgoer. As an adult I continued at the same church. Eventually we were married, and Rae and I then went to the same church.

I took an average share in the responsibilities and activities of that church, and for a long time I was a member of the Parochial Church Council. With that, the social and administrative commitment increased. Yet I never came to any real knowledge or understanding of the person of Jesus Christ. I have no recollection of the service at which I was confirmed. I have no thought to reduce the significance of my fairly considerable involvement in the life of the church over about twenty years. That activity will undoubtedly have made its mark on me somewhere, but I wasn't aware of it. I was then standing in a different place, that of one who didn't know Jesus Christ as Saviour.

Living in Walborough with the church on the doorstep, I still had absolutely no inclination to go to church. There were friendly nods with the very likeable people who passed our door to go to church, and I was glad to support the church in odd ways, but there was nothing that attracted me. Yet now I had a burden for Walborough Church!

St Marks, Walborough is a large church and one of the most important in the district. Upon entering the church, which was always open, the first and most important feature to be seen is the font, said to be one of the most beautiful in the country. It dated from about 1160. The Norman aisles are very impressive, and then on through the altar rail one is reminded that they are the memorial to one man's service for 40 years as vicar – a far cry from the three different priests that were in charge during our relatively short time living in the village. The oldest part of the church is away on the west side. The access to this was by a dark and difficult route behind the organ, and I had frequently prepared the way for my visitors to get access by opening doors with obscure catches, by signalling the step and by finding the light switch. The reward for the effort is what we called the Saxon Door. It was distinguished by its tympanum. The lintel was most clearly Saxon, and this consisted of an enormous stone rudely carved with animals and in particular what appeared to be a cat and a dog. This was always an object of special interest because these animals were upside down. I never heard any explanation of why that was. Surrounding the tympanum there is a stone triangular frame crowned by a grotesque bearded figurehead. The tympanum itself carries an assortment of saltire crosses of all sizes.

After moving in 1971 my wife and I established what can be called a loose connection with the church, and we soon became friendly with Bill and Rita, the retired Anglican clergyman and his wife who lived just outside the village. Bill often took services in the church but, apart from one funeral, the first time I heard him preach or take a service was after we had moved away in 1980. They were a kindly caring couple who represented to me just how I thought Christians should be! I remember that we had many lovely dinner evenings with them. We had good conversation and I was struck always by the fact that we didn't say grace before the meal! Bill came from a clergy-family and was brought up in the Brontë Rectory at Haworth; so I used to think Bill had made a great deal of progress from the stuffy ideas of those days and even from his own generation! But I came unstuck one evening at somebody else's house when Bill and Rita were present. The host said grace, but I had already dipped into my soup! Anyway, God's timing is better than our own, and the first book I ever read on what God is doing in these days was given to me by Bill. It was 'When the Spirit Comes' by Colin Urquhart.

I regarded the church as a neighbour on one side of our house. The Vicar, when there was one, was a good neighbour in his Vicarage on the other side. My wife took her turn in the roster cleaning the church floor. For my part, my interest extended on one occasion to attending the Annual Church Meeting. I remembered from my old church going days that this was open to all members of the Church. It seemed to be a well-attended meeting, and I was hardly qualified to speak upon anything that was discussed. This false humility on my part must have appeared as reserve and shyness for it transpired that I had unknowingly been elected a member of the Parochial Church Council! I had not realised that there were no 'public' present except me, and perhaps in accord with the ways of the past, all present were, in a 'shorthand' way of voting, elected as members. The first PCC meeting of the new year immediately followed the AGM. I was on my feet getting ready to leave whereupon my next door neighbour, the Priest-in-Charge, became quite intent on persuading me to stay on in the job in spite of the misunderstanding. It seemed that the vote of the Annual Church Meeting had been taken and just could not be overturned! But really I had no objection. It felt quite funny to be on a PCC when I didn't go to church. I still didn't go! I don't suppose my attendance record was in any way unique!

I wish I could say that I added something worthwhile to the life of St Marks Church, but I cannot. One day during that single year of office one of the young members of my family expressed surprise that I hadn't seen the human bones in the opened tombs in the churchyard. So I went along myself to have a look. I didn't know how common it was to see such sights, for I had never looked in churchyards before. As far as I recall that is all I ever reported upon in my year as a member of the PCC! Today the churchyard is very different. It is beautifully maintained. Walborough has seen a new dawn.

On rare occasions I did go to a service in the Methodist Chapel in Walborough. I found this a small, warm light and friendly place compared to its enormous Anglican counterpart. I found the informality very acceptable and John, a local farmer, was closely associated with this Methodist scene. Bill and Rita were the clergy pair I readily recognised as 'my sort of Christian'. John was their counterpart among the lay people. He was another living next door to the church as we did. I didn't understand what made him tick but I couldn't fail to notice the high standards he applied in his life. Although one of the most successful farmers I have met, he never worked on Sundays. It always appeared he had come to grips with life, his farming work always seemed to be finished in good time, and he had time to help others and to talk about current affairs.

I cannot bring forward with much clarity or certainty *why* it was that my time in Walborough was a disastrous one. The diviner I had consulted had no doubt about the reason! It is true that my wife and I had five road collisions near Walborough, all with other vehicles, within nine months of moving there. Also it is true I spent much time laid up after the final accident and was pretty well confined in the house and unable to drive my car. That was the big road accident – accident number five – that was to change my style of life in so many ways. I lost my job and its secure salary. Next instead of concentrating on how to manage money for the company that had employed me, I moved to the idea of managing money for myself. So the rot set in still deeper!

I have related previously that the burden for Walborough grew out of the pendulum diagnosis obtained for the church. It stemmed also from my encounter with Moral Re-Armament at Caux, and that aspect was something I had shared with my friends in Walborough. I was even closer on the heels of my clergyman-friend Bill in Walborough in March 1982, when I had my conversion experience. After various conversations, I took the bull by the horns and told of my anxieties and of the so-called black ley-line supposed to run through the middle of Walborough church.

What I remember most about one lovely evening, soon after I was born again, in Bill and Rita's half-timbered cottage was the Holy Communion Service. In ten years of friendship together, God had been little talked about. Bill was a man of few words, but the time had come, still not for very much talk, but for the bread and wine. He could safely trust that we would welcome what the Lord had ready for us, and Bill slipped away into his office to prepare. Getting on for midnight, the rest of us were beckoned to join him. I don't remember if I ever did previously take communion, even once, in Walborough. But I was taking communion in

Walborough now, and in a private house. Here was another way to end a party!

Links were continually being forged between the villages of Walborough and Fulbury and my new church in Kidderminster. Visiting preachers from my church were invited to the Baptist Chapel at Fulbury where my daughter attended. They were then not very familiar with 'tongues' at Fulbury, and based upon my new experience of tongues I was telling my daughter Sue all about it. Daughters don't readily believe all their fathers tell them, and Sue's reaction to my description of this supernatural gift was that it was impossible. So I showed her next a reference in a book I was reading, and she still would not accept the idea. I believe God was in control and the very next Sunday Sue came home from the Chapel and said, 'Dad, Mr Tolley got up and spoke in tongues.'

It seems there was no interpretation given, and this caused me to question a little. Then some weeks later I went to one of the Bible Study Meetings at Fulbury. I had never before met this elderly gentleman, Mr Tolley. He was there too. I told him the story of Sue who hadn't believed in tongues. His face lit up. He said he felt compelled by the Lord to give the message in tongues, and he could see now what the reason had been. The message had come as a complete surprise; but perhaps a good reason had now been found!

In those small Bible Study groups at Fulbury there always was a time of free prayer. There was much in common with my own church fellowship, and I was thankful that Sue had been led to this place so early in her young life. All this was while I was being led in directions well away from the Lord. The consequence might have seen my children on the other side of the spiritual divide. However when I came on the right side in that spiritual war, my daughter was already there.

Sue's friend, also a member of the fellowship at Fulbury, was the daughter of our neighbours next to the church at

Walborough, Jane and Brian. Through that connection, but more as an antidote to my chat about MRA to Jane in the previous year, I felt led to visit and make them a present of Colin Urquhart's book, 'When the Spirit Comes'. Everybody seemed to have been recommending the book to me. I had it from Bill, my clergyman friend, and now it was going back to Walborough. I believe God was saying, 'send the book' and I had the thought to *give* it in order to be sure it wouldn't come back!

I had no hint that Jane and Brian would even welcome the gift. What I did not know was that God had His hand on them too! They had very recently been visited by some friends, Geoff and Maureen, who I had met at Walborough in the past. Now Geoff had recently gone into the Church and was a curate. It seemed God had used the visit of those friends to touch Jane and that is what had happened. Geoff had suggested 'When the Spirit Comes' to them. They *hadn't* read it; and now here was a 'confirmation' by the copy I sent them. A new Christian relationship with Jane was born.

Had my years in Walborough been time wasted and a time of chances missed? That must have been true as I ventured further and further outside of God's will. But it soon became clear to Jane and to me that a new dawn in Walborough was about to break. Like our house and John's farm, Jane's was the only other house next door to the church. We had all been neighbours around the church, with this enormous landmark and its churchyard positioned in the middle of us.

12

Walborough – A New Dawn

Although we had not seen much of each other in the last years of our time at Walborough, we had had some good times with Jane and her husband, Brian. Our children were growing up at the same time, and we had done much together. Now there was Jesus in the relationship. Jane had been born again – and at the same time as me.

Jane was one of the church stalwarts over many years, and with all of her five children she had served in many ways. Brian was like me! Indeed the discomfort at even being inside the Walborough church building was intense! He thoroughly disliked being in the church for whatever reason.

Jane had been growing in the Lord. Her new associations were at the Baptist Chapel in Fulbury. I had been going to the Elim church. In particular ways she was picking up the same threads as me, and we each had come to hear of the Church of England parish of St John's, Harborne in Birmingham led by Canon Tom Walker. Jane had recently been converted there, at the same time as I was being converted in another church, and we had resolved quite independently to visit St John's. I now knew my own new church but I had not seen anything of the people in other churches which had been renewed and who were using the gifts of the Holy Spirit in a similar way.

I first went to St John's in July for a Sunday morning service. I had never before been in an Anglican church that was anything like this one. The modern building had been erected in 1960 to replace the original bombed in 1941. Then the building was enlarged in 1974 under Tom Walker's leadership to give the enormous and apparently very efficient church complex seen today. Large permanent signs are displayed to each road frontage: 'Jesus is Lord'. I believe those signs would have spoken to me about the fellowship of Christians within, even without the recommendation to the place that I had.

Inside there was little of the paraphernalia I had been accustomed to in Anglican churches. I too had been a member of a church with a brand new building in the 1960s. I had always thought it a fine church construction, but then I had been on the PCC throughout its building! (It has now been completely demolished having been found to be structurally unsafe). Many of the traditional ornaments had still been in evidence in that new church, but not at St John's. On this particular day the centrepiece at the front was a blackboard and a display of visual aids. Excepting the cassocks and surplices worn by the ministers, the denomination would have been unknown.

It was a friendly place, crowded with perhaps six hundred people. Conversation with the neighbours in the pew was easy and almost inevitable. The service itself compared little with the Anglican services I had known, but this might have been due to the changed prayer book as in so many churches. It was freer, with some arm waving, but unlike in my own church this was usually delayed until the last verse of a chorus! I was encouraged by the freedom I did see, and by hearing personal testimonies spontaneously given out by members of the congregation. When I introduced myself to Tom Walker, there was just time for him to tell me he had a cottage on the hills that overlook Walborough. Bells started to ring immediately!

I determined it would not be long before I went back to see Tom. Jane and I would go together! That was easily arranged for the following Tuesday – the day St John's have their mid-week 'Open to God'. Jane invited farmer John, the other 'neighbour' of Walborough church, to go along too. John, a Methodist leader, was also connected with the fellowship at the Fulbury Baptist Chapel. He had been my daughter's Sunday School teacher during her early years there. He also was taking a look at this new Anglican scene for the first time. There were well over a hundred people. Tom recognised us and the three of us were able to share with him something of our burden for the church in Walborough.

Out of all this Tom said one thing that registered very definitely on my heart. He said he knew that there were very many churches in that area that would 'never do any good until they were delivered'.

All three of us were blessed by this time with Tom Walker and those in his fellowship, and our conversations in the car went on long after we had arrived back in Walborough. We were looking ahead in expectation of the wonderful things God would do in the village. Our thoughts were turned to the vacancy for the Vicar of Walborough. The Priest-in-Charge had retired on 31st May; and actually, at the same hour we had been in Birmingham, the leaders of St Mark's Walborough were meeting to formally consider candidates who had already been interviewed.

I was still a very new Christian, and in July 1982 there was a great deal of learning to be done. As fast as I was reading a book or hearing the Lord in any way that seemed relevant, I was sharing it with Jane. Many books passed that way, but an extraordinary thing was happening. I had believed her husband Brian to be tolerant, but possibly distant from all that was going on. Like me he had not been a great reader of books. Yet I learned he was ahead of Jane in getting through all the books I was sending. It was not to be long before he was sharing as enthusiastically as the rest of us.

Jane was invariably very busy with her many interests, but one day in July I was making some late arrangements to

111

go to a Prayer Group in Redditch. An hour or so before I was due to go there, I drove over to Walborough somehow knowing Jane would go with me; I believed it was right she should go. In the course of conversation I mentioned I was on my way to Redditch, and it was immediately clear she would go too.

The Group was at the home of Jo and Harold. They were very old friends, and my wife's friendship with Jo dated back long before our marriage. We had seen little of them in recent years. Maybe I avoided close encounters because I knew they were Christians! However this was another 'Prayer and Praise' evening of the sort I was now very familiar with. As ever it was encouraging to find yet another place where the Lord was moving in this exciting way, and where the Gifts of the Spirit were being used.

We were a very long way from my home, and much further from Walborough, but when we took our places in the crowded room there was an old friend of Jane's seated next to her. During the time of prayer I thanked the Lord for the way the Holy Spirit was moving in Walborough and for His blessing on those who were working for Renewal in that place. Then, following immediately, Jane's friend began:

> 'Just as our brother was beginning to speak I had a picture. It was of a church. An old stone church. And all the windows were boarded up. But the place is being opened up and new life is going to go into the place.'

I did not note the actual words, but they were something along those lines; all those in the room praised the Lord.

I was in no doubt by this time that the Lord had a wonderful plan for Walborough; given an obedience to His will I would see something more working out. It was an exciting time. There were many people praying for the Lord to take a bigger hand in Walborough. They had prayed regularly at Fulbury for many years. Canon Tom Walker was asked for prayer. My own church group was praying. We were praying at Redditch and prayers were being said at the inter-denominational group at Kidderminster where people from Walborough had attended. That may be the tip of the iceberg; there were perhaps more prayers said for the renewal of the church in Walborough than I can ever imagine.

Throughout the summer there was a great deal of sharing of what God was doing. That was the inter-regnum period, with no priest at St Mark's. It was a slacker time in the life of that church and the opportunity was taken to draw members of the church into fellowship. Brian and Jane organised a successful 'Praise and Barbecue' evening. There was a long way to go, but new relationships were being made, a spirit of praising the Lord was emphasised, and there was good fellowship between Fulbury and Walborough.

Bill was there. He told me that 1 Samuel Chapter 3 had spoken to him. I could not wait to get home and see what this scripture said. Then with the enthusiasm of a '5-month old' Christian, I couldn't resist replying to two verbal sentences with two written pages! I suppose Bill has been a Christian for well over 70 years, and I was still counting in months! I didn't want to draw too heavily on his comparison of me to Samuel but I needed to be as frank and as wise as I could just as Eli had demanded of Samuel in the Scripture.

There was a New Dawn in Walborough. They were exciting times, and there was still much to look forward to. The new vicar was due to arrive at St Mark's in December. The inter-regnum would be over. But much would happen in the meantime, and God's plan would be worked out further.

13

Anglicans All Around

My family were all members of the Church of England. We had been baptised. Whether we had been to church or not, whether we believed or not, we were members! That is what I was told! The first service I attended after learning how John met his awful death, was in a local Anglican church. I couldn't remember hearing 'healing' much preached about in a church before, but that day the theme was 'Christ the Healer'. Healing and deliverance were preached that morning. To my absolute surprise I also found the clergyman taking the service had been our vicar some sixteen years earlier. He had joined our last church just at the time of our moving to a different parish when I decided to call it a day after twenty years of churchgoing. There I was. I had been sixteen years in the wilderness. Sue, our daughter who he had christened was now sixteen years old, and we discovered he was our neighbour once again.

Just when I was urgently starting to look into the dangers of what I thought was my own healing power, the Lord had used our last vicar from the last church we attended sixteen years before in order to bless me with the Good News that Jesus was the Healer.

Everything I had been involved with seemed to point to this subject of healing. Not only had I covered much ground in counterfeit healing, that search had taken me to Jack Mowate, our Anglican curate friend who had a healing ministry.

Now as a born-again believer it was not long before I heard from a friend about another Anglican church! 'Oh Roy. You're interested in healing. There's a healer preaching on Sunday.' This preacher turned out to be a man from a 'Sanctuary' in the south of England. I had previously been with him at a weekly gathering in the church. Now he was given a spot in the 6.30 p.m. main Sunday service. On the previous occasion I had not been a Christian. Now I was, I was doubtful about the realm in which this man was working. I was able to take advantage of an invitation to meet him informally. Although my knowledge was limited as a new Christian, it was soon quite clear to me this was the sort of healing I should have nothing to do with. I most certainly would *not* go to the Sunday service! We were nonetheless able to talk freely and frankly and at the end of it I was given a copy of the extensive notes he used for talks to potential healers. I was able to have these checked out carefully by my pastor and he spelt out the error to be seen in almost every one of the twenty long pages. An Anglican clergyman friend agreed with his assessment. My conclusion had been reached by a simpler method, but here I had valued and measured assessments from two ministers with quite different backgrounds.

I found the Anglican church at large such a mixture with much 'tolerance', a place for everybody, and almost anything goes! That was how it seemed to me. 'Why not change it?' I thought! 'Doesn't the Lord want it changed?' I could understand tolerance of *people*, but how could the Church of England tolerate such so-called *healing*? I had been, at age 45, somewhat delayed in grasping the Good News of Jesus Christ, but how could clergy tolerate such variety? Where was the discernment of Spirits? These were the questions I asked myself.

My discovery of the supernatural started with the power of Satan. I didn't know it *but that is what it was*. Many clergy don't know it, *but that is what it is*. The common denominator in the theology has shifted so far from historical Christianity that it can become barely recognisable as Christianity before causing alarm. Added to that there is the individual freedom of the minister. So, not believing that Satan can 'heal', and believing that all healing is good, ministers are finding a way into the supernatural with Satan's help. How many believe in Satan anyway? I didn't!

The first book my pastor gave me was Trevor Dearing's 'Supernatural Healing Today'.* In one chapter he refers to what he calls 'An Important Distinction':

> I had not long been involved in ministering healing when I realised that a vital distinction had to be made. I discovered that not all supernatural healing is Christian. 'Spiritual healing', 'faith healing', and 'divine healing' are not interchangeable descriptions of the same phenomenon. The term 'faith healing' puts all the emphasis on our 'trust' in anything or anyone. It says nothing at all about God. Christian healing, however, is not merely about a psychological attitude which can produce good results. It affirms the necessity of an openness of spirit and soul to the God and Father of our Lord Jesus Christ.

I could see it was those who picked their Scripture who were missing out on this essential understanding. I found that, far from believing or not believing in Satan, the minds of so many professing Christians had not been addressed to the question. Many don't believe in him, and for them there is every danger. Then among the Christians themselves, in every denomination, I was to find an alarming lack of discernment between true Christian healing and psychological attitudes and techniques. We need to discern the 'important distinction' to which Trevor Dearing refers.

As a new Christian I was learning about the 'church' I had grown up in. Indeed I seriously considered if I should return. Jack Mowate had shared with me about the controversial book recently produced by Anglican scholars, 'The

*Published by Logos, Plainfield, New Jersey, USA (1979) and printed by permission.

Myth of God Incarnate'; with my general observations over the years, this prompted the question of what is being done about it. I learned that the Church of England has little or no provision—at any rate no formal provision—for removing priests from the Church's ministry unless they have been guilty of breaking the law in a criminal sense or for gross heresy. Since the latter is seldom proven a man can continue in his ministry even though he may be ineffective in preaching the Gospel and carrying out his pastoral duties.

The best analysis I found on why a churchman should consider resigning was by the Rev Dr William Oddie:

> It is *not* to be guilty of bigotry to say that a priest ought in essen tials to teach what the Church teaches, or that he has as Bishop Charles Gore put it, an obligation 'really to believe in what he (in the creeds) solemnly professes to believe, in terms which are deliberately unambiguous'.'

The Anglican tradition has always tried to narrow its doctrinal requirements to a minimum of beliefs it considers truly essential. And that *has* to mean that those requirements are met, at the very least, by those in Holy orders. In the words of Bishop Gore, himself a great champion of intellectual liberty:

> We must be very gentle with scrupulous and anxious consciences. We must be very patient with men under the searching and purifying trial of doubt. But when a man has once arrived at the steady conviction that he cannot honestly affirm a particular and unambiguous article of the creed, in the sense that the Church of which he is a member undoubtedly gives to it, the public mind of the Church must tell him that he has a right to the freedom of his opinion, but that he can no longer, consistently with public honour, hold the office of the ministry.

Dr Oddie went on to say that one thing is depressingly

*Daily Telegraph—20.12.82.

certain. It was that the 'public mind' of the Church of England would remain firmly silent on this issue. In Churchill's words 'resolute only to be irresolute, adamant for drift'. I concluded that as long as that tendency continues the vitality and effectiveness of the Anglican Church will be seriously impaired. It was some months afterwards that the appointment of a secular unbelieving professor as Bishop of Durham confirmed very well the Anglican Church's situation. To set right the situation, what possibly can be done?

On becoming a Christian I repented of, and renounced, all my occult activities one by one and I had burned all the books and items collected on the occult side of the supernatural dimension. I cancelled my regular order for 'Psychic News' at the local store. The only church newspaper with a name that I could recall was the 'Church Times'. I didn't know its large circulation and status as the leading Anglican paper, but I believed it would assist me to see what the church was doing. After buying 'Psychic News' I thought it might restore my respectability at the newsagent's shop!

Reading the 'Church Times' each week was a wearying exercise for an up-and-coming evangelical! After six months I said 'enough is enough'! As soon as I decided to cancel my order my eyes came upon a headline – 'MEDIUMSHIP "POTENTIAL GIFT OF HOLY SPIRIT"'. This seemed to be the view of the Churches' Fellowship for Psychical and Spiritual Studies (CFPSS). Some months previously at the last minute I had decided after all *not* to attend a conference of the Churches' Fellowship. I believed it wouldn't be right. I remembered being tempted by seeing that a bishop would be speaking. I was still at the stage when, even as a new born Christian, I believed it must be alright with a bishop involved! It was now clear the CFPSS did believe mediumship to be potentially a gift of the Holy Spirit.

My message was clear. I wrote to the paper:

'Reader beware! Christian beware! There are no spiritual planes, as many would claim. There are two kings, two kingdoms and two sources of supply for the needs of the spirit.'

That is the theme of my story in this book – a look at the spiritual battleground of which so many are totally unaware. The ensuing correspondence, both privately and through the columns of the paper, showed the level of unawareness of this war. The private correspondence was to further convince me of the existence of more than I imagined who were ministering healing and not using the power of God.

I found it was not always easy to determine, from the words and style an individual used whether the necessary awareness was present. Some knew Jesus as their personal saviour and were aware of the dangers on the wrong side of the spiritual dimension; some did not. That was the important categorisation. Some did know the Lord in that way but had not stepped out in His service filled with His Spirit. Some had already been drawn into enemy territory without realising it, and were in real danger; others were ignorant of the truth that is to be found in His word. Some that were really seeing the whole matter as essentially intellectual were perhaps relatively safe – at any rate for the time being! Others were, as I had been, in immediate danger. They were the ones who have discovered something entirely consistent with their idea of 'good works': 'It is exciting!' 'It is supernatural!' 'It is for good!' 'It must be from God!'

I was into the Anglican scene once again. The 'Church Times' and the ample letters I received reflected thinking in the Church of England; they represented truth and error in a demonstrable way. I learned a great deal from the private dialogue – sometimes three way – prompted by the columns of the paper. I heard from a vicar's widow who unknowingly was in considerable danger. And I heard from another vicar's widow who was the opposite! She wrote:

Your letter in the 'Church Times' gave me great joy. I am sure you are right. Thank you for writing. I despair when I read what is put over in the paper. What has happened to our good theologians?

'What has happened to our good theologians?' Whatever the vicar's widow had in mind as she wrote, the next issue of the 'Church Times' contained the answer.

Just 25 years before, Godfrey Ashby had sailed for South Africa to become a missionary, as he put it 'to proclaim Christ to the heathen'. He was working for the Society for the Propagation of the Gospel (SPG). Now a bishop, he had recently spent time back in the UK. Like me he was asking, 'What has been happening whilst I've been away?' I was readily able to identify with what he wrote in the 'Church Times':

First, there is a widening gap between what we of the Third World Churches understand by mission and what it means in Britain (social action, aid to the under-privileged and social development)*. In the main, African and Asian Christians understand their faith in terms of Jesus Christ, Son of God, become man for our sake, sacrificed for our sins and alive, powerful and risen. To them Scripture is authoritative.

They are not fundamentalists in an intellectual or militant sense; Scripture has the authority for them as it had for the Church Fathers; they accept it as it speaks to them; they are willing to have it applied. But, if you say or imply that it lies – then they begin to wonder if you are not the one who is lying.

In the main there is no problem of atheism; there are very few atheists in Africa; the problem is that of seeing Christ as Saviour as distinct from a distant God and pantheon of ancestors – and there is a certain amount of confusion in that area.

Now, what does a Christian leader from Africa or Asia make of English Church life, where it is embarrassing to talk of personal commitment to Jesus Christ, dangerous to admit to his being Son of God and inviting contempt to invoke the authority of Scripture? One Priest from the Scottish Episcopal Church admitted to me that one of the external partners could not be exhibited in public because he would look like a theological dinosaur.

So what has happened, broadly speaking, is that the churches

*Author's brackets.

of Africa and Asia have experienced revival and renewal and some of them have experienced persecution. They have found themselves proclaiming Jesus as Lord and Saviour, claiming the infilling of the Holy Spirit, and have used the Scripture to teach and build up the faithful – and all this irrespective of tradition, High and Low, USPG, CMS. All have been infected – with, of course, many pockets of dying Christianity and many moral lapses.

They have also taken the problems of the world around them seriously, bearing in mind that they are in the Third World and know more about starvation in Karamoja than they know about the Brandt Report. (Question – has Africa heard of the Brandt Report?)

On the other hand, whilst there is renewal and revival in Britain, particularly among groups of lay-people who have found a living faith in Jesus and have experienced the power of the Spirit in them living and are longing to grow in their faith and to be given a lead by their churches, the picture is very different. I hope I am not too harsh, but this is what I see – and I am an Englishman by birth and upbringing and was ordained in South-wark Cathedral. British Churchmen have become embarrassed by the Christian faith and British people are profoundly bored by it. The result is a Church that has abandoned evangelism profoundly to a few professionals and has concentrated on issues that do not concern personal faith or commitment.

The subjects most debated in Church circles are either matters such as opposition to apartheid in South Africa or the Soviet invasion of Afghanistan or the Brandt Report; or esoteric matters that titillate the intellect or please the current concerns of the media – Prayer Book revision, ordination of women, schemes of reunion. Now these are all weighty matters, but decisions taken on them one way or the other are not going either to convert a single soul to Christ or to set the Church aflame with the Spirit.

There is also little authority. Bishops tend to be committee-bound and benevolent; priests have to rely on their reputations for being trendy or kindly or organisationally talented or witty, exciting speakers; and the laity flounder, and, if they happen to be seized by faith in the living God, do not know where to turn to for encouragement. Few dare teach from Scriptural authority in case they are refuted by the authority of the latest German commentator or British theologian.

I am sorry, mother Church, but this is how I find you – in the main. There is a very serious division growing among Christians fostered and encouraged by the Powers of Evil themselves (and they themselves are not the subject for polite conversation in the British Churches today).

It is not the division between haves and have-nots; nor is it the division between Catholics and Protestants; nor is it the division between South Africa and the rest of the world. It is a division between those for whom mission means commitment to Jesus Christ first and then involvement in the world's problems under the power of the Spirit, and those for whom mission means involvement in the world's problems first and maybe commitment to Christianity afterwards.

In 1958, the great missionary societies knew what their goals were, though they often floundered about in their methods. I get the impression that now there is no such certainty – the uncertainty of the mother Church has affected her missionary activity and unnerved her overseas outreach as well as at home.*

It was good to read that for it seemed he was at the point I had arrived at. The main theme of the rest of the article was the divided view on the meaning of mission – the Bible or the Brandt Report! This was where the change had come. New Age or New Birth? I had moved on from my time of close involvement in politics. I had moved from the worldly solutions and was unashamedly into the *only* solution – the one that was found in Jesus. Was it, as it seemed, that the Anglican Church was leaning now almost entirely on the solutions previously left to politicians? I concluded sadly that the answer is 'yes'. I was beginning in 1982 to discern the difference between the Church, the bride which Jesus is preparing, and the people Satan was grooming – New Age people focusing on peace, the creation, self-effort and co-operation, and eventually one-world government.

In politics, I used to speak of two sorts of people – those who 'care' and those who 'don't care'. As a Christian my division was between those who were walking with the Lord and daily being filled with His Spirit, and those who

* Bishop Godfrey Ashby. 'Church Times' – 29.10.82.

were not. In politics, I had learned that it didn't make you care more if you were a Member of Parliament. Now, I had no reason to suppose a Bishop was more likely to be filled with the Spirit than anybody else. Bishops and clergy had one thing in common and that was a good intellect. Looking at the route to Jesus I had travelled, and at the way I had missed the path for so long, it seemed that intellect could be a real disadvantage reflecting only the complicatedness of the ugly world man had made.

There was one encounter with my old church which was significant for its contribution to my assessment of the Anglican situation. In our Elim service one weekday, there was a guest preacher – a Baptist minister from Birmingham. His subject was the vision for the body of our church fellowship and it tied in with the theme of commitment that had been preached in the church for a couple of years. I had to decide within the next few weeks whether to commit myself as a *member* of the church. I was seeking guidance on what my decision ought to be. I didn't like the thought of leaving Elim; but was my place back in the Church of England? I was still trying to weigh up the situation that night.

No two services are ever the same, and on that occasion Mick Reynolds invited anyone with anything to share. Gale stepped forward at once. She was moved near to tears and quite distressed, but she spoke in a measured way. I had heard her preach in the church and this night her message was again perfectly clear. Her sixteen year old daughter, Ruth, had been that day, along with 250 other sixth-formers, to a conference held at the Bishop's Palace. The speakers had included an Archdeacon, three other clergymen, a divorced mother, a homosexual and a single mother with a daughter to support. Gale had been horrified at the views expressed by these people from their privileged platform positions.

As Bishop Ashby had written 'the meaning of mission is changed' and it seemed that instead of the Gospel, these children (inevitably — in these days — a product of a secular society) were treated to an assortment of views on divorce, homosexuality and sex-before-marriage. There was free beer in the lunch-break irrespective of age. Most teenagers haven't found Jesus Christ, but also many have still to discover divorce, sex-before-marriage and homosexuality. The sixth-form day out was a liberal and a practical exercise, and a reflection of the Anglican church I was rediscovering.

14

Discerning of Spirits

As a new reader of the Bible in a lively Spirit-filled church, and as one who had experienced the counterfeits of God's gifts, it was natural 1 Corinthians 12 would be one of the more familiar chapters of scripture. Now, exactly seven months after my conversion, the Lord was to lead me through a quite extraordinary week.

Friday had been a fairly unspectacular day. I spent part of the morning with my solicitor on some business matters and he was prompted for some reason to ask what plans I might have for a field I owned and which adjoined the church at Walborough. I told him I wouldn't mind letting the village use it at some time if the right sort of purpose presented itself. I hadn't thought much about it; it would be a Christian purpose of some kind, but I had no idea what or why.

When I returned home, George Miller (the evangelist who had led me to the Lord), and his wife Hazel, were having lunch with my wife, and we all shared the first sight of the correspondence still running in the 'Church Times' and delivered that morning. There were on this occasion three letters in the series on healing I had started; one of them was another of mine in which I had quoted extensively from 1 Corinthians 12:

'For to one is given by the Spirit the word of wisdom; to another the word of knowledge by the same Spirit;

To another faith by the same spirit; to another the gifts of healing by the same Spirit;

To another the working of miracles; to another prophecy; to another discerning of spirits . . .'

Saturday was eventful, and the event of the day was a multi-denomination conference on evangelism. The Bishop was the Chairman and the principal speaker was Tom Walker. It was on that day the Lord first spoke to me about homoeopathy. I began to discern in my spirit that it may be occult. I didn't even know what homoeopathy was except it was a medical therapy. On Monday, in the evening, it was to be Tom Walker's meeting again, in another place where I regularly attended and where this man happened to be speaking yet again. That day I received a letter from Margaret, who lived in Liverpool. She had read my letter in the 'Church Times' about 1 Corinthians 12 and was desperately appealing for help. It wasn't at all clear what the problem was but I replied right away that unless I heard otherwise I would be at her house at 10 o'clock on Wednesday.

The three of us (Jane, John and me) who had met with Tom in the summer went to the meeting on Monday evening with a good crowd of other folk from Walborough. I hadn't forgotten Tom's spontaneous words: 'So many of the churches in that area will never do any good until they are delivered.' By this time Jane's husband, Brian had been baptised by the Holy Spirit and he was there too.

Tom Walker chose as his text, 1 Corinthians 12.

The next day, Tuesday, I heard from Margaret who was delighted the visit to her was planned and at the church in the evening, talking with the pastor, a lady who I recognised but did not know, entered at the other end of the hall. 'I believe she will go with you. She has a deliverance ministry,' he said. 'And *she* will probably baby-sit,' he said, motioning to another lady who again I hardly knew and who was standing at the other side of the hall. Within five minutes it was all arranged for the journey. I could see the value of all the people who make up the body, and who were all essential. My prospective young travelling companion had three children all under five, and the mission wouldn't have been possible without full provision for them.

The next morning Diane and I set off for Liverpool. She had washed a line full of clothes before I arrived at 7.30 a.m. with Lisa who I had collected in order to mind the infants. Diane's husband Bill was away at Bible college. More than that about Bill and Diane, I didn't know.

The steady car journey up to Liverpool provided the opportunity to get a good idea of where Diane was in her Christian walk. She was clearly way ahead of me and there seemed no doubt where the initiatives would come from when we were in Liverpool with Margaret. I told her my story and of the pastor's idea for a book (this one!) and I soon was clear that hers would make an even more remarkable story.

We arrived on time at the terraced house. Margaret had seen us arrive and she came out to welcome us. I knew Ben, her husband, worked as a bus driver and that was where he was that day. Sitting comfortably in the living room, I still didn't have any idea what Margaret's problem could be. I introduced Diane as a fellow member of our church, but bearing in mind the difference between our ages, reckoning my contribution to the 'Church Times' and considering the lead I was giving in the conversation, it will have taken Margaret some time to realise I was after all just the 'warm up' man! I didn't need to do much talking except to steer this eloquent lady in the direction of telling relevant things about herself. Margaret was middle-aged. She was a graduate and was studying on a post-graduate course. She was a regular attender at her Anglican church. She seemed to be involved in its life and activities, and there were piles of paper on the sideboard that had to be delivered on behalf of the church. She was articulate and her haphazard story touched on one or two problems. Even so in the course of the first half hour it seemed to me there was nothing extraordinary. Certainly she hadn't identified anything particularly significant. Although she spoke of some ESP experiences she had, there was nothing that appeared to support the urgency of the plea for help in the letter. Indeed it was a package of problems that would be reckoned as mercifully small by great numbers of people in these days.

Diane spoke hardly at all as I conversed with Margaret and tried to steer the dialogue towards the relevant questions. In other words, what *was* the problem? I didn't know. Had I been there on my own I would have been close to the point of saying a prayer and taking my leave!

At a convenient pause, Diane joined in: 'The trouble is that you don't know Jesus.' For the moment I was taken aback. I believed in Diane without hesitation but the flash through my mind was in anticipation of the worst sort of reaction to that statement. Here was a mature woman, a graduate and probably more than an intellectual match, a reader of the 'Church Times', active in her church probably for many years, and she was being told that she didn't know Jesus. But Margaret wasn't in the least hurt or offended. The fact was, she had a problem. I didn't know what it was. She was glad for us to go and meet her and she quarrelled with nothing. She had written the letter to me because she wanted help and she was quite ready for whatever it was we would offer.

Diane said, 'I am going to pray, and afterwards I want you to pray in the way that I will show you.' At this she led off with her prayer before explaining to Margaret how she could pray and ask Jesus into her life as Lord and Saviour. Prayer aloud seemed to be very easy for Margaret. She prayed at great length and for several minutes. As ever she was eloquent. She thanked the Lord for sending Diane and me to her, and she covered a great deal of ground. However all the time I was asking myself, 'Will Diane be satisfied with this?' Would God be satisfied? Diane had spoken few words, apart from in prayer; she had asked Margaret to ask Jesus into her life. The vital simple words had not been heard. I concluded that Diane would indeed *not* be satisfied as on and on the prayer flowed from Margaret's lips. At length she stopped. 'But you haven't asked Jesus into your life,' Diane told her. Margaret really wanted to get there.

'I'll try again,' she told us. And off she went! Again it was eloquent. It was long, and as ever Margaret seemed to be easily taken away from the points at issue. At least it seemed better than the last prayer. Whether Diane would accept it I just didn't know. In due course the prayer ended.

I don't remember what were Diane's exact words, but they were something like, 'That's a lot of rubbish; you've been deceived.' I was really taken aback this time! What would Margaret say to that? 'You did not pray that prayer. It was the spirit of deceit,' Diane went on. She looked Margaret in the eye and there was no doubt in the mind of any of us that Diane meant what she said. It was about this time that it dawned upon me that the Lord was managing this whole situation. Diane was speaking with the authority of the Lord. Not only that, the Lord had been speaking clearly to Diane about the specific problem areas in Margaret's life and about which there had been little or no clue from the conversation or from Margaret's prayers. But Margaret was not at all daunted. 'Well I'll pray it again,' she requested. 'No you won't!' Diane insisted. And there could be no arguing. 'You have the spirit of deceit and you have to be rid of it,' she said. At this, Diane glanced at me, and in a fraction of a second I flashed back my willingness to assist her with the deliverance. Margaret took no persuading. Unlike Diane, and apart from not *knowing* Jesus, *I* didn't know what Margaret's problems were.

Diane stood up leaving Margaret where she was sitting. She gave one instruction to me. She said I should pray in tongues throughout, and she turned to address the spirit. She first bound the spirit so that it could do no more damage.

When she came to ordering the spirit of deceit out of Margaret my eyes were closed, and I continued with my prayer until my curiosity could be contained no longer and I opened my eyes. I saw before me a contorted face pulled into the most hideous expression that could possibly be imagined. Margaret, although seemingly glued to her seat, had her arms and fingers outstretched as far as she could reach. My eyes should not have been closed at all, and I did not close them again. The spirit strained and pulled at Margaret's body and after a few minutes she was slumped in relaxed relief, thankful that the spirit had left.

Diane had discerned another spirit – the spirit of fear. Margaret was willing, and off we went again. Margaret's body was now slumped to the floor. She was in an awkward, twisted position but no attempt was made to correct it, and when Diane addressed this spirit there was soon screaming at a strange pitch such as I never before had heard. It was a piercing scream and, I am sure, quite unlike Margaret's own scream. As the screaming began my glance went in the direction of the window. There were buildings all around. However it would hardly have mattered if a face had appeared outside. I was aware of the presence of the Lord, and if anybody had appeared at the window it would have been in His will. The spirit screamed and screamed and screamed. It seemed it would be never ending, but it did not matter. At length the spirit left, and once again the subject slumped with relief.

'But there is still the spirit of the hate of men,' Diane told her. Still game, but ever more weary, Margaret indicated her assent. Once again, having carefully but without ritual gone through the preliminary prayers, Diane took authority in the name of Jesus, with the protecting power of His blood. Working according to Scripture and binding the spirit, she proceeded to order it out. This one was not so easy. 'Come on, come on; it's no use hiding,' said Diane in a perfectly normal voice. 'I know you are there.' Again there was this same screaming. But this time there was no sudden relaxation, and I wondered if the spirit had left.

That was the end. On the journey home Diane shared with me some of the things about which the Lord had spoken; and she shared that the spirit of hate of her father did not come out. Margaret remained sitting on the floor for several minutes as she recovered her strength. 'Now, will you ask Jesus to come into your life?' Diane requested. It was not in doubt. Still eloquent, but it was quite a different prayer, so differently spoken. At about 12.30 Jesus truly came into her life. After hugs, before lunch, we were on the road out of Liverpool on our way back. The Lord had been there with the three of us throughout. He had provided Diane with all the knowledge – direct!

The previous day God had given Acts Chapter 16:16–18 to Diane. She had read these verses even before hearing about the lady in Liverpool. What a confirmation it was!

'And it came to pass, as we went to prayer, a certain damsel possessed with a spirit of divination met us, which brought her masters much gain by soothsaying:
The same followed Paul and us, and cried, saying, "These men are the servants of the most high God, which shew unto us the way of salvation."
And this did she many days. But Paul, being grieved, turned and said to the spirit, "I command thee in the name of Jesus Christ to come out of her." And he came out the same hour.'

Diane shared that with Margaret. For my part I still had the one question that puzzled me. Why had Margaret written to *me*?

'In my own life, after dangerous adventures in the occult, I found the answer was to be born again by inviting Jesus into my life and really knowing Him; and regularly to call upon Him to refill with the Holy Spirit.' This is what I had written in the 'Church Times', and that is what Margaret had read. 'I wrote to you because you seemed to be so sincere,' she said.

That evening was the regular weekly house group. Mick Reynolds led it; he took 1 Corinthians 12 as his text. At the conclusion Mick, and Val his wife, prayed for each of us to receive spiritual gifts.

Jane from Walborough was visiting the group that evening. It came to my turn, and in his prayer Mick prayed that I should know the gift of discerning of spirits. He prayed in an informal way, and referred to my role of a sort of assistant during that morning in Liverpool. He prayed that I would receive the gift for use myself on some future occasion. With that, I thought no more about it.

After the meeting had ended, Mick and Jane were getting better acquainted. She was telling him about the Satanic-looking signs in Walborough church. Once again I didn't think twice about it, and the same was true when I heard Mick say to Jane in what seemed like an off-the-cuff remark, 'I don't suppose there have been any tongues in that church for a good few hundred years!'

I was thrilled Jane had decided to come to that meeting. We had shared a burden for Walborough; also I was able to share the blessing of my morning in Liverpool with her. For me, Wednesday had been quite a day.

Very soon after waking the next day the clear thought was in my mind, 'Go to Walborough Church'. I was quite clear it was from God. As the morning went on I became more certain that I should go to St Mark's Church to find out what God wanted to show me. By lunch-time it was irresistible and off I went in the car. It was many miles from my home and I prayed in tongues all the way. This was something I quite commonly did when in the car on my own. On this occasion I was praising and praying in rather a more lively fashion.

I had no thought to go mooching around in the church. I had no thought about what God or anybody else might show me when I got there. I was in His hands and He would show me whatever He wanted me to see or feel. It might be a cold draught around my neck, it might be some Satanic sign, or it might be anything; I was clear in my mind that the Lord would have to show it me, and there was no thought of combing the building like some sort of surveyor or Sherlock Holmes. I had heard of these Satanic signs myself. I could have looked out the books any time and done my research! Indeed I knew who had the information if I was interested. I was concerned, but such interest was inadvisable and hadn't seemed right. It didn't seem any more right or relevant this day; I was simply driving to the Church as God had led.

A mile or two away from my destination I unaccountably paused from the tongues, claimed the gift of discernment for Walborough Church, accepted the gift and thanked the Lord. In a second or two I was into my tongues again. I parked the car and went into the church. As I did so it was quite clear in my mind that I *wasn't* going to pray when I got inside. I had gone into the church with visitors and tourists many times in the past, and with no thought of praying! But this time it was different. Although I was now a Christian I wasn't going in there to pray but in obedience. As to the reason, I didn't know!

I was full of expectation as I walked around – the porch, the famous Norman font, the north aisle, the south aisle, the chancel and over the whole of the main area of the church. What *was* I here for?

I knew precious little about churches. I reckoned every visitor I showed around already knew more than I did. They always seemed to see things I never noticed. But this time I *was* seeing the details. There seemed little remarkable about that; I was on my own. I was walking around, obviously looking around about; I noticed in particular many of the *ugly* things. I felt comfortable enough, and the overall appearance of the architecture struck me as very attractive indeed. But for the first time (though it is mentioned in the Guidebook that is always available) I was noticing the lone carved grotesque figure perched over one of the columns in the north aisle. I was seeing for the first time the detail in the carving of the font, and even of the relatively modern pulpit. Yet I saw no significance there. It was a case of *having* to look at *something* as I wandered around! Then I began to pray in tongues. I did this often, anywhere and almost everywhere. Not part of any plan I knew, but here I was, praying in tongues in St Mark's Church. I think my mind must have flashed back to Mick's comment the night before. 'Perhaps a *thousand* years without tongues,' I might have thought!

I rarely discussed the subject of 'tongues'. I must have been well aware of the popular reaction; Paul said this was the least of the gifts. I could only agree, and I have never stood *in Church* to give a word from the Lord in tongues. I had praised and prayed in tongues but that had only served to edify myself. That is, until the day before in Liverpool. Many an authority on the ministry of deliverance has said he would be unhappy to minister without the support of prayer in tongues. The enemy cannot bear the sound of tongues, and there was no doubt in my mind that the enemy had been at work in St Mark's Church. As Tom Walker had said to us, 'Many churches in that area will never do any good 'til they are delivered.' So around the aisles and chancel I walked, speaking out my tongues. I paused when I came to see marks I thought I recognised, and I was trying to make them out more carefully. Then I stood back, and just as I began my tongues again I heard a noise. It was the big door opening, and in came two ladies. They were spending the day visiting the churches in the area. At once their presence was a distraction. I was in the chancel and some way from them. Normally I would break the silence with a welcoming 'hello', but they were a bit too far away for that. As expected I saw them make their way from the door to the font.

Very quickly I realised they would want to see the Saxon door; and immediately the message shot from my brain to my heart! 'Ah the Saxon door. That's it! Why didn't I think of that!' They could not have easily found the Saxon door without my help. I had walked around for several minutes and I hadn't been near it. The Lord had really shown me nothing up to that time and the thought of showing them the Saxon door made me very excited indeed.

The Saxon door is on the west side of the church tucked away behind the organ. It is little used and predates the church which is Norman. I had seen it dozens of times and the special feature was the lintel formed by an enormous stone some five or six feet long and 18″ or so square. It is specifically Saxon and what I remembered was that the animals on it were upside down. No-one knew why! It was beautifully smooth-looking just as it might have been when it was put there 1,000 years before.

I moved towards the visitors, and after an exchange of greetings I proceeded to open one door, then another door to let the light into the inside porch, and then the door itself into the outside porch. Then, with the visitors alongside, I put on the light by which we could easily see the lintel and the tympanum above. I raised my arm to point out the much-prized monument. Immediately we could all see that it was broken into two pieces. It was not just a crack; it was fractured through the middle.

One of the visitors, who worked for the Diocese in the Cathedral, observed what was a new break. Instinctively I put my finger to the crack and to my slight embarrassment a piece of the stone fell to the ground. The visitor was about to do the same when I saw a larger piece of the fracture ready to be dislodged! I said I had been praying, but that I didn't realise I had been praying that hard! Albeit a pointless remark we exchanged some good humour. The lady, introduced as 'from the Cathedral', said she would report what she had seen, and the two of them were on their way. What could I have said to them?

The new vicar had not yet been installed. I met two more church ladies. Both were on their way to arrange the flowers and I went back to the church with them to point out the damage. One of the ladies had seen the stone in perfect condition at the weekend.

I then called on John, the farmer who had been with us on Monday. John was, of course, familiar with all that had happened recently in Walborough and Fulbury. He had been with us in the summer when Tom had shared about the need for deliverance of many churches in the area and I had shared with him my burden that dated back to the diviner's diagnosis for the church. I knocked on his door without any thoughts as to how to introduce such a story. 'John, they say the Lord's got a good sense of humour. Is that right?' That was the best I could do to start off with. Off we went back to the church.

The church and its door is a show-piece, and maybe I had shown that door to visitors 30 times in ten years. That is all, and it is hardly what could be described as a busy procession of visitors. It will be the same for the other neighbours, John and Jane. However John had taken someone to see the tympanum and lintel the previous Saturday. It had still been in its pristine condition.

Next I went to see the other neighbour, Jane. She had shown the Saxon door to a visitor on Sunday. Once again, it wasn't damaged.

Over a cup of tea we waited for Brian to return from work. John, Jane and I had all heard the message on 1 Corinthians 12 from Tom Walker on Monday. Brian had been there too. Unlike John and Jane he hadn't seen the stone recently, not for five years or more. Although born again a month or two before, he still didn't care to go into the building of St Mark's at Walborough. The break was a sign to each in different ways. In Brian's case it was again a different one. In quite an extraordinary way he too had met the stone in recent days. Brian told us that on Monday night, following Tom Walker's message, he was unable to get much sleep and had spent the night tossing and turning. He told me he had a dream. He dreamt about the church at Walborough and that he was asked by the leaders there to turn the stone the correct way around. Off we all went once again to the church. Brian had not seen the stone for years, but, apart from the break, it was all as he saw it in his dream. He knew building principles and he was able to give his opinion that there was no evident natural explanation for the break. It wasn't a load-bearing stone. Brian was in business as a builder in stone and renovator of old buildings. In the village today the Old Vicarage is a Christian Centre, where

Brian and Jane live and run it.

I went to bed that Thursday night with the clear thought that I ought not in any way to try and push this extraordinary story along. If the Lord could arrange people to see the stone in perfect condition, to dream about it, and to say nothing of breaking it, then he wouldn't need me or anyone else to go telling everybody about it. I was now curious about the signs and symbols and the upside-down animals, but once again it didn't seem that God needed me to go researching into books or anything like that. As I began the day on Friday my thought was to leave Walborough alone and not risk getting drawn into any ideas in my own strength.

It was quite early in the morning and I was sitting in my office in a comfortable chair. There will be no more of Walborough, I said to myself as I got up to make a start at my desk. Lying there was the Bible. I picked it up and sat back in the armchair again. I had never really read much Old Testament. I had picked at it at various times and I had read Genesis. I had read the *New* Testament through twice since becoming a Christian. Now the book seemed to open itself at 2 Chronicles 2 and I began to read about the preparations for building Solomon's temple. On through to chapter 7, I came to the dedication of the Temple and to the time when the Lord appeared to Solomon:

'But if ye turn away, and forsake my statutes and my command ments, which I have set before you, and shall go and serve other gods, and worship them;

Then will I pluck them up by the roots out of my land which I have given them; and this house, which I have sanctified for my name, will I cast out of my sight, and will make it to be a proverb and a byword among all nations.

And this house, which is high, shall be an astonishment to every one that passeth by it; so that he shall say, Why hath the Lord done thus unto this land, and unto this house?

And it shall be answered, Because they forsook the Lord God of their fathers, which brought them forth out of the land of Egypt, and laid hold on other gods, and worshipped them, and served them: therefore hath he brought all this evil upon them.' (2 Chronicles 7: 19–22).

137

Was this relevant to the situation? I didn't know.

Once again the next day, Saturday, I was brought back to the Old Testament, in the same way as the day before. Earlier in the week, I had received a letter asking if I wanted to sell a field there next to the church. It lay on the desk awaiting reply. That was the field my solicitor had asked about. My Bible opened at Jeremiah 32. Again I was *not* saying, 'Right Lord I'm opening my Bible NOW. You make sure I'm at the correct page!' It was rather that I opened the book, and the first words I saw were 'Jeremiah Buys a Field'. I read the scripture. Here I again quote from the Authorised Version:

> *Thus saith the Lord of hosts, the God of Israel; Take these evidences, this evidence of the purchase, both which is sealed, and this evidence which is open; and put them in an earthen vessel, that they may continue many days.*
> *For thus saith the Lord of hosts, the God of Israel; Houses and fields and vineyards shall be possessed again in this land.'*
> (Jeremiah 32: 14–15)

Was this relevant to the situation? Again I didn't know for sure, but I thought I'd better keep the field!

Then on Monday I went over to Walborough to see a few people. I had a bite to eat with John and Jenny, leaders at the Fulbury Chapel fellowship we had come to know through our daughter Sue. By this time they had heard about the broken stone and had been to take a look. John seemed interested to know what was the meaning of the symbols and the animals. My pastor had asked that question, and now here was another mature Christian asking the same thing. I didn't know as I had turned away from the question. Now I couldn't contain my interest any longer, and quietly resolved to head directly for the Birmingham Central Reference Library immediately I had left them.

I had researched in that library before on a variety of subjects. It was efficient and always came up with something useful. It is a modern spacious library with specialists and computer referencing in each department. My first port of call was the Religion and Philosophy Department. The staff were most attentive, and mid-afternoon on a Monday was clearly a quiet period for the library. It was clear what I wanted. I had photographs of the symbols and signs that were even clearer than the stone itself. I wanted to read anything that could be found relating to pre-Norman church buildings. The Fine Arts Department was drawn in. Then the History Department. All produced nothing. Two hours, with numerous staff beavering away into good filing and record systems, were absolutely unproductive. I still marvel that this should have been so.

Driving out of the centre of the city, somewhat despondent, a new idea came to me. 'Go and see Tom Walker. Now!' Instead of heading for home I made for Harborne and went to his church. I didn't expect to find it dead and closed up. Indeed it was open with all sorts of people about the place and connected with the evening activities. I got Tom's home address and off I went and knocked at his door.

It was just a week since he had preached 1 Corinthians 12 to our group with 15 or so from Walborough and Fulbury. Tom was in my thoughts too because I believed he would give me the name of an Anglican vicar in Liverpool who would be appropriate to continue the ministry with Margaret. Tom knew the ideal man in Liverpool to continue with that. It transpired that he lived not a half-mile from Margaret; subsequently I heard from him that he was seeing both Margaret and her husband regularly each week and helping them grow into a real and living faith.

Tom Walker was clear with three points for the village situation. Firstly, he saw that the break in the stone was a 'breakthrough' for the village. Secondly, he had had a vision that the village would be the centre for the lifting of the darkness that he knew existed in much of that Clee Hill area. Thirdly, he said Satan's symbols and signs were frequently upside-down, and there was therefore no need for research in the library.

In ten days it seemed that many questions had been answered. I don't believe I would have found the answer to any of them in a library!

I had been a full-time 'searcher' in the occult realm, and immediately on becoming a Christian I became a full-timer in God's kingdom. The Lord continued to occupy me. He was to answer many questions. Sometimes He would pose questions I wasn't interested in, and then lead me to the answers!

Such an example was with Rock music, and He showed me that this, even when described as Christian with scriptural lyrics, was demonic. He did that in a single day and the story is told in the next chapter.

15

'Rock' and the Switchblade

At one of our weekly housegroups, the pastor recommended a book. It was 'Rock' by Bob Larson. This subject was one in which I had positively no interest. I had once been at a village hall 'disco' when a friend suffered a continuing hearing deficiency. I didn't have Rock around me! We had no neighbours to play it loudly and our teenage children didn't seem to have any particular interest in it. 'Rock' gave the Christian view. The Pastor was saying 'get it', and so I bought it.

Bob Larson is a musician as well as President of Bob Larson Ministries in Denver, Colorado. I started the book one Saturday in the summer sitting on the lawn at my home. I was still there on the lawn when I finished the book. It is an exposé of the rock culture as a dark world of occultism, violence and perverted sex. It provided an analysis showing how mind and spirit could be influenced. Once I started, I couldn't put the book down.

At last, towards evening, I finished the book. And almost immediately, the telephone rang. It was a young man called Gabriel. I knew his elder sister who I had seen the day before. I knew Gabriel had an exciting life. It was a life in the world of professional rock musicians.

I didn't know Gabriel personally. However he was now telephoning me for help. He told me he was very frightened. He had just found himself sharpening a flick-knife (a 'switchblade') and he had it in his hand. He said he could actually see two of these knives although there was only one.

141

He said there were Eagles record covers on the wall that frightened him, and he didn't know how they had got there. Also, he said, the record player was playing 'Bat out of Hell' and he didn't know who had put the record on the turntable. The music was frightening him. He told me the clock had been moving backwards and that he was seated cross-legged on the floor with no clothes on and with the switchblade in his hand. He spoke for about an hour. Although he was scared, his words were well measured. I ended the conversation with a prayer. I had made notes and collected my thoughts as best I could and I told him I would be in touch again before eight o'clock.

It seemed an incredible experience to receive a telephone call like that as soon as I had finished reading such a book. For the first time I had seen the terrible dangers latent in rock music. 'How has it come about that God has got me on this job?' That was the question I was asking myself. Certainly He had me do my homework and get it finished in the nick of time!

Gabriel had phoned his sister before phoning me. She had said, 'Ring Roy.' I knew his elder sister very well indeed, but why had she said that? The answer is that I had talked with her two days before about the two spiritual realms. Why? Well certainly it isn't something I did very readily! I had called on his sister Clare and her husband quite out of the blue as I had done many times before. Admittedly I hadn't been a Christian more than six months, but I had never as I recall, discussed God or any spiritual subject with them on any previous occasion. This time I had been prompted by a story Clare told about Ted, her teenage son. She told me what Ted had told her that very morning.

Ted had got up much earlier than usual. He had been very frightened and wanted to relate what had happened. He had been up into the early hours as usual. Then at about half past one in the morning Ted became aware of a presence alongside him. There was nothing to see but he could sense someone very close to him. Ted was petrified

That is bad enough, but through our music we can be led more directly into the occult.

In one day I learned that rock music, at any rate much of it, conveyed a good deal of Eastern thought, and that occult themes such as in The Eagles' 'Hotel California' are abundant in the rock scene. The teachings of the 'Moonies' are strange and horrifying to many of us but they are more easily grasped by those brought up on rock; also teenagers are more vulnerable than the average adult in the face of Satanic idealogies.

'What the lyrics say, and what the singers do!' That doesn't mean you are immune if you don't hear or don't understand what they say. There is no immunity for not knowing what the singers do. Some of the lyrics are clearer than others. Some songs are better known by parents, for example the very popular 'My Sweet Lord' by George Harrison of the Beatles. Who *is* 'My Sweet Lord'? George Harrison wrote the foreword to 'Bhagavita-Gita as it is', an introduction to the Hindu religion available in England!

When I had spoken to Gabriel on the telephone, it was clear he needed help right away. In order that we could visit Gabriel together I met up with another Christian who had some experience of problems like this. We headed north and reached Gabriel's smart city flat by eight o'clock. He told his story with frankness and it was one which was unmatched by anything my friend could recall in his many years of counselling and deliverance; it is a story that is not told here. The record covers on the wall were by the Eagles. They were still there. The record player was in the corner. The record 'Bat out of Hell', that had frightened him, was by Meatloaf, the other group with which the Lord had prepared me in my afternoon reading.

The three of us spent two hours or so together. It was an evening of ministry that I believe will not quickly be forgotten by any of us. At the end of it Gabriel prayed and asked Jesus Christ to come into his life. I slipped out to the car to get the copy of 'Rock' I had read that afternoon. I gave it to him. In one day the Lord had introduced me to rock. But more than that, he had given me a very intensive one-day course.

God had put rock music on my heart. I had already discovered by my own experience how the likes of me could come into the bondage of Satan. I could look back on the mixture he had prescribed for the intellectual 'searcher'.

There were subtle ways too for the youngsters. It wasn't just sex, drugs and porn; there was the music too.

This most unlikely interest – rock music – continued, and my ears pricked up at anything connected with 'Rock'.

I heard from a schoolboy of a rock record played backwards, and of gruesome Satanic messages that could be heard. I was able to obtain a tape from the United States. This was a message by a pastor and the Lord had put it on his heart to expose the enemy involvement in rock music. I came to see that there was perhaps no better way than rock for Satan's evangelism of young people. The Beatles had been at the centre of developments. One tape carried part of 'Revolution 9' from their 'White Album'. Played forward there was heard 'number nine, number nine . . . ' Played in reverse there was heard 'turn me on dead man, turn me on dead man . . . '

I heard the lyrics of 'Hells Bells' by AC/DC. They came over as if it was Satan himself speaking: 'I'm a rollin' thunder' was the introduction. Then I heard 'My lightnin's flashin' across the sky. You're only young, but you're gonna die. I'm gonna take you to Hell. I'm gonna get ya. Satan'll get ya.' AC/DC have another record called 'Dirty deeds done dirt cheap'. As I heard on the Christian tape – 'that just about sums it up – Satan's dirty deeds are being done dirt cheap'.

Among the selection of backtracking examples was a very clear and startling message on the LP 'Face the Music'. It was from the number, 'Fire on High'; played backwards, the following lyrics can be heard:

The music is reversible but time is not.
Turn back, turn back, turn back, turn back.

148

That was recorded by 'The Electric *Light* Orchestra' or 'ELO'. Satan can change himself into an angel of *light* (2 Corinthians 11:14). Satan reverses everything. Satan turns good into bad. He seeks to make God's work his own. 'The *White* Album' is *pure white* on both sides of the sleeve with no coloured lettering – only the lightly embossed words, 'The Beatles'. I purchased both this and the record by The Electric *Light* Orchestra, *black* records dressed up as *light* and *white* that only *God's light* can expose.

I bought one more item – another set of LPs. Its characteristic was that every record had sold a million copies and there on the front were to be seen the pictures of the 'super-stars' that a month or so previously I had never heard of. Have *you* heard of Alice Cooper? Alice Cooper is male, and his exhibitions on stage include biting off chickens' heads. In the record 'Alice Cooper goes to Hell' the devil is characterised as 'The greatest; number one'. Cooper has said that the ultimate is to commit suicide on stage.

Then there is KISS. Is there a KISS poster in your child's bedroom? When I first mentioned KISS to a young friend of mine I found she had bought one as a gift for someone. KISS is famous for posters. Millions of posters have been printed. KISS also have a record about this God of Thunder, the God of Rock 'n Roll. On it we hear, 'I was raised by a demon, trained to reign as the one.' It concludes 'I gathered darkness to please me and I command you to kneel before the God of Thunder – the God of Rock 'n Roll.' KISS means 'Kings in Satan's Service'. Also on this 'Million Sellers' cover was the picture of Meatloaf, famous for the 'heavy metal' rock music, and used in Satan's service where Gabriel was concerned.

Why was I, a Christian, buying 'The White Album', the Electric Light Orchestra LP and the 'Million Sellers' album? That is a question I *did* ponder both before and after I stepped into the record shop. I had been a 'searcher' once; and wasn't that all finished? Hadn't I burned all things connected to my occult adventures? I believed God had a burden for exposing the rock scene, but as a new Christian I suppose I wasn't sure. I knew that bright ideas, however well-meaning and seemingly effective in a worldly way, would surely fail if God was not in them. However, as I went into the shop my idea was to buy one or two records I had heard reversed. Then I would reverse these originals for myself to make a more effective way of witnessing. I would make my own Christian tape. There would be my own words and the original records. So I believed my motives were OK.

As I entered the shop I felt an oppression with a headache in a way I don't remember experiencing previously. I speeded up my prayer as I moved around the display counters. There was no fear, it was a dark shop and I felt I was in another world. I had never been in such a shop before. I was glad when it came time to leave.

Off I went and I drove my car. Without braking I ploughed across a 'stop' sign and into a main road. Another rammed into me. Both vehicles were written off as scrap.

Up to that day I had regularly spent an hour in fellowship with the Lord before beginning the day. On this day I had been tired. It had been done half-heartedly. I stayed in bed. In other ways too I had got off to a bad start.

The following day I saw my evangelist friend, George Miller. I had been 'open to the enemy from the beginning of the day', he said. I had not put on the full armour of God that was available to me. God had saved me, and all those involved from any injury. A lesson had been taught. There had been spiritual warfare. Satan, already defeated in Heaven by the death of Jesus for me on the cross, had lost another battle here on earth.

At the time of the collision the car was loaded up with a record player, two cassette recorders, amplifying equipment and the three records I had purchased in order to make my tape. None of this was damaged. My own Christian tape exposing rock was made, and the Lord undertook for a speedy insurance settlement on the car that was more than satisfactory.

The first time my tape was played in a Christian group, it had to be stopped half way through. Such was the effect on one lady who had heart trouble. The leader of the group was a doctor. He explained that the beat of rock was in a different time to the human heart. 'In fact, it is the exact opposite,' he said.

Rock and disco, perhaps next after TV, are Satan's subtle way of introducing children to the New Age. Happily our own children were not devoted to this form of entertainment. Yet *I* had been introduced to these techniques for 'switching off', through meditation and strobe lighting. I believe, throughout, the Lord had His hand on our children just as He had His hand on Rae. Her own testimony in the next chapter tells how somehow she was steered clear of many things we both now understand and recognise as occult.

Our car was written off and we thought we had lost it for ever. It was a very comfortable, old and not-very-valuable Fiat. It was 'RAE 16 S', a 'personal number' on the car when we bought it. Rae was fond of the car and said jokingly it showed her name and age! It had become a mangled wreck. Months later we heard from a garage, just when we urgently needed a car and had no money. 'We've got a car that will suit you,' the man said. It was the Fiat. It had had two owners since us – the insurance company and the garage – yet we found the registration still in our name. It was still RAE 16 S and it had been rebuilt with parts of other damaged Fiats. It looked better than ever. The price was much less than the insurance settlement. The Lord had once again finished what the powers of darkness started and brought a happy ending. The car was bought. We were back on the road with RAE 16 S!'

16

Rae's Testimony

At the age of fifteen, my parents, believing that the school that I was then attending was not up to standard, decided to send me to another. They thought that it would be good for me to stay as a 'weekly boarder' so that I could concentrate on working for my 'O' levels away from the distractions of horses and friends. I had a great deal of work to do to reach the required standard in one year.

Of course all the other girls in my class had been at the school for years and had formed their friendships, and I felt very much 'left out'. Also I was not used to my freedom being so restricted, and from Monday to Friday when I was 'let loose' for the weekend, seemed an eternity.

I had always been given 'Scripture' lessons at school, and reading the Bible was an everyday occurrence. I never had any trouble believing what I read.

Every evening there was a time for prayer, and one day when I felt particularly unloved, I asked Jesus to be my friend. Certainly for several weeks afterwards I felt very close to God, but the significance of what I had done was not to dawn on me for over 20 years. Looking back it is very clear that Jesus did just what I had asked him to do, and there was to be a protective hand on my shoulder from then until the present day!

There have been many things that I have been asked or encouraged to do over the years, and there has always been that hand seemingly holding me back. Some of the things that I might have got involved with were Yoga, ear piercing, healing (the wrong sort), Tarot cards, fortune telling, not to mention the numerous things that even my husband was to try to persuade me to take an interest in.

When Roy became involved in the occult (although I had no idea even what that was!) I became more and more frightened. I knew that what he was doing was wrong, although I couldn't have explained why.

Happily my friend was still with me, even though for long periods of my life I had ignored His presence; and at the height of my anxiety, around the time of John's death, He was to prove that He was right there, and knew my most secret thoughts.

It seemed that Satan had saved his trump card for me at this time. When Roy returned from the 'Christian' Spiritualist church, telling me what he had been told about the beautiful leather book, the inscription inside it, and the unusual hand of the owner of the book – was I interested?!! This was undoubtedly Mr Wyborn, the much revered friend of my paternal grandparents – now *that* made me sit up and take notice. But I was to be grabbed hard by that hand on my shoulder.

The following evening we heard of the horrible circumstances in which John was found. I went to bed, set to stay awake for hours with anxiety. But there was a voice that said quietly in my ear, 'Trust me.' I had no doubt whatsoever who it was; I immediately experienced a 'perfect peace', all worry gone, and went to sleep.

When Roy first started going to the Elim Church I was pleased, but not in a great hurry to follow him. So often he had found something new which was 'marvellous', only to disappear into the memory within a few months. Only after this new thing had stayed 'marvellous' for about six months, did I venture to accompany him. Of course, I had heard all about the wonderful things that happened each Sunday, so I was not surprised to see people raising their hands in praise and dancing in the aisles! Indeed I felt quite 'at home' even on my first visit – so much so that I went again and again and on every Sunday from then 'til now! It gradually dawned on me what had happened when I was 15 at school all those years ago. I had been saved not only from Hell, but from all sorts of other things in this life too!

My first big event occurred during the 'flu epidemic of our first winter at the 'Elim'. George Miller was at home this particular Sunday, and was taking the Gospel service in the evening. I nearly didn't go, as I was sure that I had caught the dreaded bug! So there I was, feeling pretty rotten. 'Praise the Lord however you're feeling,' said the Pastor! I couldn't sing – my throat was too bad. Every time I tried I coughed, so I gave up trying! Near the end of the service George was saying, 'Now all who want to be saved – come to the front.' Nobody moved. 'All those who wish to be baptised in the Holy Spirit.' 'Well,' I thought. 'Yes, but another time when I'm feeling better!' 'All those who need healing; come on now, all of you with 'flu!' Dozens got up and went to the front!! Including me. When I arrived there everyone else was singing a chorus – I'd better try! Can't be the only one standing here silent! I sang – no cough! I carried on singing, but by the time George had worked his way along the row to me there was no sign of the 'flu, but I felt a bit stupid! After I had explained to George that I seemed to be healed already, he said, 'Well, what else shall we do then? Are you baptised in the Holy Spirit?' I answered, 'No.' 'Would you like to be?' he said. I was surprised to find myself answering 'Yes.' So there I was feeling a definite touch of God and about 12 inches off the ground. After it seemed ages, George persuaded me that all I had to do was open my mouth and I would speak in tongues. What me? Impossible! But I did and I do – amazing!

Amazing indeed have been many things over the last year. Amazing and exciting – but there has been heartache too! Satan still tries to 'upset the apple cart'. Disagreements between Roy and I have been more frequent than at any time since our marriage – Satan seems to be trying to bankrupt us too, which is sometimes difficult not to worry about.

There have been unusual blessings too! God seems to be very interested in our son David's motocross activities — sorting out seemingly insurmountable mechanical problems and providing money from nowhere for repairs! My personal 'welcome back' gift is unusual! My little horse, who has always been a bit of a problem and most unpredictable, started winning prizes! In fact since the day that Roy started going to church he was won or been placed in almost every competition that we have entered, whether it was dressage, show jumping or cross-country. The Lord obviously knew I was on my way back to Him!!

17

Alert to the New Age

The early days as a Christian were not easy. Rae, my wife, has testified to that. Yet they were exciting and promising for both of us. Her testimony is of one who was alert to the New Age. She could not put her finger on it, nor articulate it, but she identified the things I had come into after 1980 as having a great deal in common. Moral Re-Armament, Ecology, CND, Psychic Healing, Pendulum Divination, the Occult. Indeed they are all part of the New Age movement, that growing zealous band of well-meaning people being united together leaving out Jesus.

I discovered that the New Age movement is not a bureaucracy or an organisation but a network of social and spiritual movements. Each one is self-sufficient. Not one of them is essential to the whole, but the movement is an evident source of potential power and the network as a whole is greater than the sum of its parts. I found that behind it was Lucifer's desire to be worshipped as God. As Jesus prepares His bride (the Church), Satan prepares his counterfeit in the New Age movement which will be ready to receive him when he comes in the flesh. I looked back on my life with its involvement in, for example, the United Nations movement on the one hand and the occult on the other, and I could see writ large what was so evident when I took a close look at the groups making up the movement. In fact there are tens of thousands of such groups and I was able to look at some of the principal ones. There was a focus on man and the creation (rather than the Creator). There was a marked evidence of occult involvement in the groups, even if only those in the higher echelons were involved and aware of it. There was a focus on 'Peace' – the peace the world seeks to bring and not the genuine inner peace the Bible promises to those who follow Jesus. New Agers seek for the very plausible idea of unity and cooperation between the nations. The movement extends into every branch and level of society in countries across the world. Faced with a seemingly inevitable holocaust and destruction, increasingly there is greater support for the idea of the one-world government. The New Age movement is like a pyramid with an enormously strong base. It comes to a point at the top when the builders get there. Everybody is busy building and the point of focus at the end will be the antichrist in the flesh just as the Bible tells us.

As a new Christian I found a lack of awareness of occult infiltration in one place after another. I have said that I was brought up in the Anglican tradition, so on coming to know the Lord and seeing Jesus heal I was excited when I found there was a major church in London, an Anglican church, seeking to be an example with the expansion of its healing ministry. I read too that other healing outreach organisations for the Church of England had their offices in that church.

This came to mind one day when I was stranded waiting for a train at Euston station in London. I had bought one of those return tickets that only allow travel on trains after a certain time, and accordingly I was stopped at the ticket barrier. I took my bags over to the waiting area and sought the Lord's will for me in the time I had available. Very clearly I had the witness to go to this famous church. It would be my first visit and it was only a very short walk from the station.

Before going into the church I read the notices outside. I read about the crypt that was to be converted into a healing centre. I read a letter of commendation from the United Nations that was pinned up there. Already I had seen much to jar with my spirit.

157

At this time I had finished the draft for my first book of 'Warning' about alternative healing therapies. I had referred to t'ai chi in 'Beware Alternative Medicine' but had never seen it practised. It certainly isn't necessary to have a full understanding of these deceptive therapies; indeed it is positively undesirable as well as unscriptural to seek after an understanding of Satan's 'hidden secrets'. However, as a new Christian I did have some second thoughts (albeit from the devil) about mentioning things I had only read about. I had only *read* about t'ai chi.

Having digested all the notices on the boards outside, I pushed against the massive door and went inside. There I saw a class in progress. The students were moving gracefully in motions directed by their teacher. They faced one another, and it gave the impression of a graceful sort of martial art – not the vigorous 'mind over matter' movements of karate or judo, but in a similar style and much more slow and graceful. I didn't much like what I was watching. I spoke with the instructor when it was over and asked what it was the girls were doing. It was t'ai chi.

T'ai chi is the Chinese philosophical idea about the underlying unity of all manifestation, and it is supposed to integrate the personality with the spirit by alignment of so-called energies and the opening up of what are seen as higher faculties. It is said that t'ai chi developed from the more elementary idea of defence, and indeed these 'soft' varieties among the martial arts are especially dangerous and subtle.

There were still more things on the Anglican scene yet to come into my experience. Another large central London church was brought to my attention. I saw references to it in literature that came my way from occult sources.

Early one July morning it was clear I had arrived at an 'alive' church. The railings of the fashionable courtyard were covered with posters describing the many events, past and future. I read about one speaker; his subject was 'Revolution in Consciousness'. The Western world faced a

158

challenge of reversing the apparent decline of its civilisation in order to 'clear the way towards a state of happiness for its inhabitants'. The essence of the stance this speaker appeared to take was that the 'New Age' saw a 'spirit of progress' associated with the 'eternal wisdom carried forth by the oldest traditions of mankind'. Inside the church I found out more. This distinguished Monday night speaker had written books called 'The Magic Tarot' and 'The Occult Path'. 'Revolution in Consciousness' was also the title of his most recent book, and the publisher's handout described him as currently working on a 'Master Class Training Course' which recalled the esoteric ideals of our history. It would establish a 'true elite' who have integrated knowledge with understanding and experience, a group of individuals who would 'promote civilisation in the service of humanity, and restore to its proper perspective the nobility of the heart'.

This particular church seemed to be 'into' everything! It was indeed alive. Of course it had a Healing Ministry too!

It described itself as a church with a vision. It had grown from a church with a handful of people to a thriving community with a congregation no longer drawn from the immediate area that had ceased to be residential. Now they came from far and wide. The noticeboards inside provided more evidence that this was a church on the move; the 10-year plan was there for all to study, and they were not yet half way!

In my searching days, this would have been another paradise for me! 'Zen for Christians' was advertised. Zen sitting, it said, like Christian Contemplative Prayer, was a method of emptying the mind of distractions. An alternative was available: a yoga meditation class at the church. The Sufi Healing Order met in the Rectory! The congregation, and tourists by the busload, could read all about the spiritual healing available from members of the National Federation of Spiritual Healers.

The Plan document described a 'Search for Wholeness'

programme. The programme included healing nights staffed by a team of practitioners who worked on a one-to-one basis. This included spiritual healing and counselling, advice on health maintenance, some alternative therapies and 'on-going pastoral care'. It doesn't stop there!

This church was instrumental in setting up outside groups. These were to 'help' churches of all denominations in all parts of the country to see the 'connection between their religious, moral and personal beliefs and the problems of contemporary life'.

I left the church with a folder full of leaflets and papers. Even as a one-time searcher who had come to expect variety on the Anglican scene, I was astonished.

Most remarkable were the leaflets which advertised the 'Mind-Body-Spirit Festival at Olympia, London'. I scanned the programme. The big names in the psychic and spiritual world were there to be seen. Then there was one name I didn't know. He was the speaker there at Olympia that very morning. The subject was to be 'The New Age and Christianity', and the lecturer? Well, it was the Rector!

Of course there is much that is caring, sincere and well-intentioned. There is a real concern for the suffering people around the world, and a focus on 'Peace'. The church is part of a network – a 'Peace Network'. There is a search for answers and they wonder 'what lamps they can light' to help mankind find its way about in the wilderness. I could see little or no reference to scripture, but the search for peace had taken them to Einstein. They tell us that in 1932 Einstein wrote to Freud that he saw no hope for world peace until we had come to terms with our 'unconscious predisposition to violence'. I was informed that no serious work had been done in this area and they hoped to remedy this by 'lighting a lamp' – and setting up a working party to look at these 'important psychological aspects'.

One of the groups run from the church focused on 'power, energy, dynamism, a strength that is more than just physical – a strength that may include mental and spiritual power'. The index of tapes made from the speakers at the church read like a 'Who's Who?' in the New Age movement. Power. Energy. Dynamism. Strength indeed. But which spiritual power?

Here was an alive church with a Healing Ministry. It was expanding at a rate that called for administration and co-ordination. I resolved to go back and take another look, when the truth of what I had seen had sunk in.

As previously, prayerfully, but without any selection of dates or prior arrangements, I caught an early train to London. I arrived at the church at 8.30 a.m. just in time to attend the Holy Communion service. The Bishop of London was there. Her Majesty the Queen Mother was attending at 11 o'clock for a Thanksgiving Service. Armed with even more leaflets and information, I walked out into the bustle of London.

The thoughts I took with me were very clear. Sir Christopher Wren had been the architect. A previous Arch-bishop of Canterbury had been rector there. Here was still a significant church. Yet now it was clearly an important part of the New Age scene.

Many will regard the advertising of the 'Gay Christian Movement' in the church's news sheet as its most offensive feature. I believe there is more to it all than that. He who has an ear, let him hear (Revelation 13:9).

I was now being alerted to the New Age. God had got my attention. The extent of the New Age movement was far greater than ever I had imagined. There was much the Lord still had to show me. I describe more in the chapters that follow.

18

The End-Time Scenario –
The Time for Watchmen

In my early life I was motivated by what I could achieve and
by the rewards I would receive. In chapter two describing
my early days as a New Ager it can be seen that the
dominant area of my concern was money. I was a chartered
accountant. I had studied economics. I worked in the
financial departments of large international corporations. I
helped make money for them, and as a businessman I made
money for myself. Take away all the window-dressing and
that was my position. Indeed it is of course the position of
many.

Then after years of that sort of focus I came to know
Jesus. I was soon taken to the scripture in Revelation 13
about the way buying and selling is to be conducted in the
end-time. Incredibly I came to an understanding of the
international economic scene via that scripture. God shone
His light and I came to see both economics and the international scene in a new and true perspective. I was put on
my guard in this age of computers, credit and credit cards.

In the summer of 1982 I went to the National Exhibition
Centre with my son David for a motor cycle exhibition. As
we came out for lunch I held out my hand believing I would
be given a pass-out ticket. The attendant took hold of it, and
she scraped against my arm the rod-like device she had in
her hand. It was done quickly and easily, and it would have
been too late to argue. What had been done had been done!

But as a Christian I was to reflect on that simple operation. 'What next?' I asked myself. As a very new Christian I read the book of Revelation:

> '*And he causeth all, both small and great, rich and poor, free and bond, to receive a mark in their right hand, or in their foreheads:*
> *And that no man might buy or sell, save he that had the mark, or the name of the beast, or the number of his name.*
> *Here is wisdom. Let him that hath understanding count the number of the beast: for it is the number of a man; and his number is six hundred threescore and six.*' (Revelation 13: 16–18).

I knew the world was in an enormous economic crisis. I remembered banks had failed in the United States and that various states were insolvent having to be bailed out by the Federal government. I knew we were on our way to a cashless society and that there was inflation across the world that would have to end somewhere and somehow. Like the governments around the world, I had never really considered when or how. I knew that finance, commerce and government had become altogether less reliable. The scene across the world looked extraordinarily complex.

When I thought upon that number '666', I was encouraged that God's purposes seemed to be working out. Revelation told us it needed 'wisdom' – God's wisdom. Of course this is a speculative area. We are not to know God's plan. But we have heard the Word of God:

> '*If anyone has insight, let him calculate the number of the beast, for it is man's number. His number is 666.*' (Revelation 16:18 NIV)

I read that the code number of the World Bank is 666. Our society doesn't think about code numbers. Indeed I hadn't troubled to look at the code number of my own bank. I learned that the European Economic Community's computer is called 'The Beast'. I found it was located in Luxembourg and I believe my own name and personal details along with those of 2 billion others from the industrialised countries are

163

recorded there. It is not surprising to read that the code to activate the computer for cashless buying and selling transactions across national borders seems likely to be '666' with the personal numbers following. All would be on the magnetic tape on the card. I hadn't thought about the magnetic tape on my own card; there isn't much to think about because you don't *see* what's on it! Through Credit Cards we are already in the frame of mind to receive the new card – the Debit Card. I read in a popular magazine there was already a pilot scheme running in three cities in France, including Lyons; the Debit Card was being tested by the banks, a cross section of their customers and selected supermarkets.

Next, I expect to hear it will be easier to do without the card altogether. How could it be made more personal and safe? How can the authorities provide against the card being lost or destroyed?

The answer to these questions seems to be to have the mark on the body. I learned that some of the staff in the prison service in the United States have a number tattooed on their hands and that when they pass them under an infra-red scanner, doors open for them. It reminded me of my 'pass out' mark at the motor bike exhibition. I read that a laser tattoo gun had been invented that would tattoo every person in the world; and that it wouldn't be necessary for them to attend at a community centre or form any orderly queue! I learned that laser technology renders that unnecessary.

Soon afterwards I read that in Sweden, 6,000 people in a practical experiment, involving real buying and selling, have taken a mark. The mark is registered in a computer. It is a mark for life. It was painless and was put on by a 'ray gun'. It registers in banks and wherever those marked decide to shop. The shopkeeper, we are told, simply runs an electronic pen over the mark and it instantly sends the customer's number to a computer centre from where all information of their transactions is sent to their bank. No money needs to be touched.

Subsequently I received the confirmation that the mark had been given on the right hand and that the location for the experiment was the south-eastern part of Sweden. One senior Swedish bank official had remarked that he thought the public weren't quite ready for the system yet but that the government might make it mandatory in two years.

To the secular man, the control over buying and selling by the use of the card will be seen as Utopia. It will have much to commend it. Prejudices about receiving the mark didn't exist at the motor bike exhibition, and there is reason to suppose any arising with the mark to buy and sell will be easily overcome. Most crime involves cash. Drug dealing and the black market are based on cash. In theory this would all have to stop, because it would all be there on the computer record for the authorities to see.

As for governments the time of the introduction of the international card will get them off their hook! The problem of inflation, brought by their previous overspending, will be buried.

To the economist, inflation is the increase in the supply of money. It is the government that supplies the money, and it does this by printing it. Then it launches it into the system by lending it, by spending it and by giving it away. I knew that simple and accurate definition at school; but by the time I had my degree in economics I had received several complicated views of inflation. Governments the world over, reflecting man the world over, have been buying their way out of trouble for 50 years. John Maynard Keynes, the famous British economist was the influence in 1933 when the US came off the Gold Standard. Once off the Gold Standard the way was clear to print money not backed up by an equivalent real value of gold. At the same time the way was made clear for spending that couldn't be paid for. Others paid the price.

The problem started slowly. It accelerated slowly. It spread. The acceleration increased. It first hit one country then another. Each thought it could solve it. 'The problem would ease, and then get worse or spring up in another place. In the end all are in trouble. That is the serious position that has been reached.'* The world economy has not toppled – yet. Man is ingenious, until at length in his own strength, he fails. I needed to become a Christian to come back to the simple definition of inflation I had learned at school.

Lenin said, 'The surest way to overthrow an established social order is to debauch its currency.' Men with a purpose usually have a way of seeing important issues clearly. Lenin was such a man. Christians can see things more clearly too. Looking through Christian eyes, Mary Stewart Relfe in 'When Your Money Fails'† writes on the subject of inflation!

> So we see the giant wheels of commerce grinding slowly to a halt as economy after economy succumbs to the innocent sounding term 'inflation'. It is not my purpose to criticise any person, official or institution; just to inform you that it has been brought on mankind by greedy, power-hungry governments, which have chosen the one method (debasing the currency), most misunderstood by the people to bring economies to the brink of chaos.

It hadn't dawned on me that the international economy was in such a bad shape. No doubt that was because I was doing so much to help the process along. I borrowed substantial sums of money I could hardly afford to repay. I had been brought up on the maxim of my wise parents, 'neither a lender nor a borrower be', but only as a Christian could I see how, for me, for others and for countries, borrowing or debasing the currency, is something not understood in the world's scheme of things. Satan, the father of lies, has majored in this area.

Satan continues to operate, and I am not unaware of his

---

* 'Beware! 666 is Here' by Roy Livesey, BA, FCA. (Bury House Christian Books – 1983)

† Published by Ministries Inc., PO Box 4038, Montgomery, Alabama 36104, USA (1981)

continued attempts to pervert the truth among Christians who are earnestly seeking to hear what the Lord is saying. It is for that reason I have received the interpretation placed upon Reveltion 13, as to the mark of the beast in order to buy and sell, with a measure of caution. The same is true for the way the Lord has seemed to be speaking as regards the place of Jews returning to Israel in the context of the end-time scenario.

One year after I came to repentance and knew Jesus an evangelist visited our fellowship and gave a word of prophesy to my wife and I together. 'Thousands of people will pass through your big house,' he told us. By that time I had so clarified a message on Revelation 13 that I had started to prepare a booklet, 'Beware! 666 is Here'. I had heard an exciting tape about the Jews, and various things had come my way, but I am not sure I even knew there were two or three million Jews in Russia, and that, according to scripture, these 'people of the North' were relevant in the end-time picture. A couple of months later I met with an evangelist who had the same burden as regards the '666' message. When we had an unscheduled meeting I had the final draft of my booklet with me. It was about this time that I decided to travel to Brussels later in the summer for a conference at which Willard Cantelon would be the speaker. I knew from my reading that this man had taken a clear view of the scenario painted already in this chapter and that he had come to his conclusions many years previously. One way and another the Lord was keeping the Jews in my attention. The tape I heard had been by David Pawson, and next I found he was coming to speak locally. Just two weeks after that a Christian worker came to stay with us in our home. Previously I'd had no recall of the prophesy that thousands would pass through our house, but then I had the thought to share this with our visitor. 'Oh, I was just having the same thought,' she told me. Asked to explain, she said I should get a tape by Steve Lightle. 'God seems to be showing me big houses,' she said. She told me briefly of Steve Lightle's vision of Jews leaving Russia in a supernatural exodus and of the expectation that they would have to be accommodated in the face of difficulties and opposition as they made their way to Israel. The very next day I received a letter from the evangelist who had shared the '666' burden; to my astonishment she saw this Russian exodus as the first stage in the final scenario. The day after that letter, I received yet another communication – a leaflet this time called 'Let my people go'. I had no knowledge or previous connection with those who sent the leaflet. All this had no connection with my visitor who had just left; then on the third day I received the Steve Lightle tape. I was beginning to wonder if the Lord was taking hold of my house! Whether or not it would be used for Jews en route from Russia, I was being reminded that it was *His* house. It was now coming time to review the arrangements I had made for my visit to the conference in Brussels which was now only a week or so away. The surprises had not finished. I found that a principal speaker, alongside Willard Cantellon, was Steve Lightle. The name hadn't registered when I made the booking for I neither knew the man nor his message. Thus it was that I travelled to Brussels full of expectation. I wasn't to be disappointed.

Midway through the conference it was time for Steve Lightle's message, and, before he spoke, a testimony was given by a Dutch businessman. I could hardly believe my ears. His testimony was so similar to my own. He began by saying that in July 1980 he had a serious financial problem. Strangely that was the date that my story really began. July was the month and 1980 was the year when I realised I too had a serious financial problem, and when, after the peace found on the train journey from Birmingham to London, I met once again with Moral Re-Armament. The businessman proceeded through his testimony and it matched mine in many ways. In conclusion, he said, he didn't know how it had happened that after three years the bank hadn't repossessed his house to meet his loan commitment to them.

Then at last he knew why. The Lord had showed him his house would be used during the Jewish exodus. The testimony would have been completely implausible but for the wealth of similar testimonies being found in Europe and which seemed to bring confirmation upon confirmation that the Lord is to bring His people out of Russia. One way and another God seemed to make sure He got my attention!

Once again I received the message with a measure of caution, at least so far as my personal involvement was concerned. It would be no part of my idea to centre my life and plans around a prophesy, but I was tuned in to what it seemed the Lord was – and still is – doing. He had painted a scenario for the end-time that was confirmed by scripture. It seemed watchmen would be needed who would read current events in the light of what the Bible and the Holy Spirit is saying.

19

Watchman for the New Age

That Convention in Brussels in 1983 was the key to a great deal. Throughout my Christian life so far, I have marvelled at God's economy. He has used the same people over and over again, and He has often used a single meeting to settle many separate questions. That is how it was in Brussels.

The Lord seemed to be so busy with things to teach me and to show me that I never left the conference building unless I was going to bed at night. Except once! I needed to cash some traveller's cheques and I took this single opportunity to sit outside a street café with the idea to relax. Sitting at a nearby table I saw the Dutch businessman about whom I wrote in the previous chapter. He had the same testimony as my own and this seemed like a God-given opportunity to compare notes.

Seated there with our drinks, a young student came and sat alongside me. Unexpectedly my conversation was with this man rather than with the businessman, and very soon a subject came into the conversation which had not been in my thoughts for a long time – homoeopathy. Whilst I was in Brussels the Lord was speaking independently and separately to two more people in England, each in different places. The subject was again homoeopathy.

Some months previously, en route to another conference in the centre of England, I spent some time reading a new book which was described as a Christian exposé of psychic healing. Already I had the clear idea to write an exposé of alternative medicine myself and I was, as a one-time searcher in this field, naturally interested in what seemed to be the first book of its kind, taking a look at various therapies that had an occult root. It was through reading that book that I was first alerted to homoeopathy. Was it occult? The book didn't say it was, but homoeopathy had been lumped in with various therapies which I knew *were* occult. I didn't know what homoeopathy was but I certainly hadn't thought of it as occult. I had passed one of the well-known homoeopathic hospitals each day when a student at university, and I remembered it always seemed very respectable.

Then I was seated in the conference. A friend turned to me and pointed out someone who she said was a Christian doctor. 'He's a homoeopathic doctor,' she told me.

I told my friend of the book I had been looking at only an hour before. I had never heard of this Christian homoeopathic doctor. My friend gave me the doctor's name and address. God had got my attention! It seemed homoeopathy was something else on His agenda for me. Was God telling me that homoeopathy *was* of Him? Was He telling me it was *not* of Him? I didn't know, but one thing I did know, against the advice I was given in one or two places, it was no use asking the Christian doctor. I had been in Moral Re-Armament while a Christian, and I knew the only time I became competent to talk about MRA was when I had renounced it. I knew that people involved in anything occult could not be good witnesses, Christian or not. It was no time to consult the Christian homoeopathic doctor! I could only wait upon the Lord.

Several months passed and although living a long way from the doctor, circumstances brought us together and we came to know one another on a continuing basis. Eventually I believed the time was right and I shared my concern about homoeopathy with him. Still I didn't know what homoeopathy was. 'Homoeopathy is certainly of God,' the doctor assured me. It was time to wait upon the Lord once again.

The homoeopathy story was not to continue for some

months until that divine appointment in the street café in Brussels. I don't know how the conversation got started, nor do I remember how homoeopathy came into our discussion. The student pulled from his pocket an old envelope and proceeded to explain with a diagram the root of homoeopathy and how it connected with Paracelsus and the occult. He gave me what seemed like the most extra-ordinary – even for a Christian – reason for going to medical school: he had wanted to get to the bottom of this whole subject. Although the explanations were, for me, slightly complex, it seemed clear he had succeeded. He had done the research. He was quite clear in his spirit, as I was in mine, that homoeopathy was indeed occult.

Two days later I was back at home to join an evangelist who had already arrived to stay in our home. This was the same evangelist who had confirmed my message 'Beware! 666 is Here' and it was the same one who had written first with the message of the expected Jewish exodus. In the days immediately before, while I was learning from the medical student in Brussels, the evangelist had been staying with the homoeopathic doctor. By this time the doctor had become a good friend of mine. Our visitor brought good news. She had discerned the spirit of homoeopathy. More than that, the Lord had spoken at the same time, in another place, to my good friend. She told me he had renounced homoeopathy. He had destroyed the equipment and his homoeopathic medicines. I was able to share the further confirmation I had received at the same time in Brussels.

It was now eighteen months since I had come to know Jesus as my Saviour and Lord. I have said that very early on in my Christian life it had seemed clear that I should write, and that I should *warn* about holistic health and alternative medicine.

My first attempt at this had been long since completed, and in size it could only have been described as a booklet. Somehow I didn't get the prompting that it was ready to go to press, and in the meantime with the further additional information the book simply grew. Yet still the time for publishing the book didn't seem right. For one thing I believed the book needed a doctor who would write the foreword. It didn't need any such thing, but that's what I believed! Then at last the way became clear. The book needed the foreword of the homoeopathic doctor. This was the first book, at any rate in the English language, that identified homoeopathy as being occult. In spite of the evidence I had, the book needed to wait for the doctor's testimony. This came in the foreword he wrote, and the book was completed according to the Lord's own timing.

The book was called 'Beware Alternative Medicine'.* It was out in time before I was due to go to America. Shortly before leaving, I received a welcome letter from a Christian who I had never met. He wrote that if I was anywhere near Arizona I should try and meet with a Community of Evangelical Sisters. I had planned to spend four weeks in America, and only the first week was committed. I had believed the Lord would fill my time, so here was at least a start. My week's commitments were actually *in* Arizona.

When I arrived I telephoned the Sisters. There were three spare days before I was to leave for California, and my idea was that I should seek the Lord's will for the message I would give in California. No arrangements for any meetings had been made. I didn't know where I was going except that it was certainly to be California. Some of the occult I had been involved in had a Californian connection; at least it seemed right to take a message back there!

Warmly welcomed and comfortably settled in, I could indeed see Jesus in the Sisters I met there. Yet in a strange and contradictory way, from the time I arrived I was uneasy in my spirit, and I couldn't account for it. My room had been made ready with flowers and a kindly note. There were

*Second Edition renamed 'Understanding Alternative Medicine' by Roy Livesey. Published by Marshall, Morgan and Scott (Life Changing Books) and New Wine Press – 1985

fine books on the shelves alongside my bed. They made good Christian reading. I was among loving and caring Christian ladies.

I believe it was the Lord's will that at 3.30 a.m. in the morning on Thursday January 16th I became wide awake. Up to that time only two things had really registered in my spirit. First, I remembered my first visit to a Moral Re-Armament Centre. At the first opportunity I had been taken aside to watch films about Moral Re-Armament and the Founder of the Centre. Now, here in the Arizona desert, this procedure had been repeated. They were useful films, but really they were again about the Founder.

The second check in my spirit had been the Christmas tree and the baby in the manger that fairly dominated one of the common rooms. Christmas was more than three weeks past but, as one Sister put it, she really would be sorry when it all had to be taken down!

I knew the scripture about Christmas trees, and in the middle of that night I was taken to Jeremiah 10:3:

'For the customs of the people are vain: for one cutteth a tree out of the forest, the work of the hands of the workman, with an axe.
They deck it with silver and with gold; they fasten it with nails and with hammers, that it move not.'

Then I read on to verse seven:

'Who would not fear thee, O King of nations? for to thee doth it appertain: forasmuch as among all the wise men of the nations, and in all their kingdoms, there is none like unto thee.'

I could see that Satan had a plan. He had a plan for me in occult healing. God had overruled in that situation and I was born again; yet Satan had a plan for Christians too. I thought of Frank Buchman, the leader of Moral Re-Armament, a man who had a wonderful conversion experience and founded the Oxford Group which later became MRA. I thought of others in MRA today who had gone adrift after conversion through taking their eyes off Jesus. Many still loved the Lord but they had brought alongside Him those absolute moral standards. They had blurred the focus. I recalled my Christian friend and Bible teacher who the Lord had used to teach *me* so much. For twenty years he had practised homoeopathy until renouncing it and repenting of it a few months before.

God gave me the message to give in California. I presented it in different ways along with my testimony. In essence it was: 'Whoever you are, Satan has a plan for *you*.'

From what I learned about the founder from the films and particularly her book about escaping the web of deception, it seemed she would know very well about Satan's wiles. Thus it was pretty inevitable I would once again, as so many times before, find myself asking the question: was I being unduly critical? Many had accused me in that way, and indeed it was some time before I had a complete peace about exposing these errors the Lord seemed to be showing me from the start of my Christian life. Who was I to question such a distinguished Christian leader with a world reputation?

I read what Paul wrote to the Thessalonians:

'Test everything. Hold on to the good. Avoid every kind of evil.'
(1 Thess 5:21–22)

The Bereans were of more noble character than the Thessalonians. The writer of Acts tells us:

'They (the Bereans) *received the message with great eagerness and examined the scriptures every day to see if what Paul said was true.'*
(Acts 17:11)

Then I remembered Paul's reproof of Peter, the man who would later be venerated (mistakenly) as the first Pope, a man who had been around a lot longer and who had actually lived with Jesus in the flesh.

There seemed to be no question about it. Whilst showing

me the quality of the devotion of the Sisters to Him, He was also showing me error that needed to be put right. It seemed to me Satan had brought about error in two ways. Firstly, wise as the leader of the Sisters undoubtedly is, as Jeremiah wrote, *'there is* **no-one** *like the Lord.'* The focus has to be *only* on Jesus and not even on wise leaders.

The second error was in the view taken of illness. Certainly there are blessings that can come from illness, but in another of the many books, all written by the founder, placed there in my room I read that for each illness we need a specific kind of comfort. It was acknowledged that some illnesses burdened our souls whilst others caused us much bodily pain and caused us great inconvenience, but, I read that each illness had been *chosen* personally for us by our Father out of love for us and that the misery of illness would be changed into a blessing according to God's plan, if only we would accept the suffering and if only we would rest in God's hands when *He* strikes us down.

The leader of those Sisters has focused upon God's love throughout her many illnesses. But do we really have a God who *chooses* our illnesses for us and then strikes us down with them? The answer to that question is 'no'.

Jesus won the victory over illness at Calvary, and according to God's word, written in Isaiah 53:5, *'by his wounds we are healed'*.

Jesus has done it all. It is now up to us to apply that victory in our own lives. Jesus bore our sicknesses so that we wouldn't have to bear them. There in that desert retreat I reflected how different that was from Satan's plan. He makes the leader ill and hinders her ministry for the Lord, then persuades her that it was God who struck her down! Yet Satan never goes too far from the truth. He whispers that God is a loving God who takes care in 'choosing each illness' for each one of us personally.

Satan is a tempter (1 Thessalonians 3:5). Satan is a deceiver (2 Corinthians 11:3). Satan is a hinderer (1 Thessalonians 2:18). Satan is a restless lion (1 Peter 5:8). Satan is an accuser (Revelation 12:10). Satan is the god of this world (2 Corinthians 4:4). The book loaned to me on the blessings of illness gave me confirmation for the message I was to give in California.

Satan most certainly has a plan. The message God gave me was clear. He undertook for my needs in every detail. I was able to speak at fourteen meetings, including on TV, in California. The message was given to many thousands of Christians: 'Satan has a plan for every one of *you*.'

God adequately provides for us as we take up the command and do battle with Satan. Satan wants God's people to be sick. Then he wants to provide some answers. He wants to be in on everything in this world, and he gives us occult alternative therapies and harmful medical drugs.

Sickness is from Satan. The healing was at Calvary. Jesus has done it all and we apply it by faith.

Part of God's answer is to be under authority according to Scripture, and to be open to what God is saying to the Body. Yet this cannot take the place of the personal relationship, through His Word and the Holy Spirit, which God wants with each one of us.

When I shared with one of the senior Sisters what I believed the Lord had given me she told me that when she was a nurse in a New York hospital she believed, like me, that sickness came from Satan. Now with the Sisters, she said she had changed her view.

The message God gave me became the subject for prayer in my own life: 'Lord, thank you for your Word. I am a believer, not a doubter. But where I miss what you are saying, I pray you will protect me from the error that would lead me astray.'

Error is clearly a handicap to the believer. I was soon to learn that errors could often be powerfully taught. I sought to get to the root of the errors I seemed to be finding. I was troubled by the message heard from some 'Faith' teachers: 'ye are gods'. I was troubled by Man's techniques in 'Inner Healing. I was troubled by what seemed like a lack of discernment in regard to 'Signs and Wonders'. I needed discernment from the Lord. I needed wisdom too.

It was with the background of valuable teaching received from one of the well-known 'Faith' teachers that, prompted by a rather dismal-looking personal and business financial situation, I retreated once again into what I had come to call the 'prosperity scriptures'. It seemed like a 'retreat' but once again the Lord could turn it into another victory for Him. Not unnaturally I turned again to my favourite 'Faith' teacher and to the printed material received from America in his recent mailings. This reminded me of the Bible references. Once again my faith came from the message which was heard through the Word of Christ (Romans 10:17).

My faith in God to honour His word and provide for our needs came from the Scriptures, and it was just at that time I needed to make my second visit to the United States as a Christian. After an extraordinary week in America described in the following pages, I returned on the day our house had been burgled. Many valuable objects we could do without as Christians were taken. A large insurance settlement was paid very quickly and once again the Lord undertook for our financial needs in a way we could never have imagined.

The confirmation for that U.S. visit came in an extra-ordinary way. I received a telephone call from a Christian friend. Referring to some of the teaching of my favourite 'Faith' teacher, he told me: 'I thought I should tell you, the Lord has shown me that the teaching is from the spirit of antichrist.' Surprised at this, and not fully believing a word of what my friend was saying I informed him (for he did not know) that I just 'happened' to have been deeply into the prosperity scriptures. He didn't know we received the same mailings from America and he quoted from the material in order to make his point. It seemed remarkable that we had both in a sense done our 'homework' on the material he was using as an example, but nevertheless we agreed we wouldn't *discuss* it. We would both *pray* about what he had said.

178

Some days later, thinking I had better do the right thing, I rang my friend back and told him I had prayed and that I was quite happy about the teaching. Then I prayed over the telephone. During that prayer the Lord gave him a scripture for me. It was Ezekiel 3:6 though he didn't know what the verse said. Some days later we met and he asked me: 'Did you read on to verse fifteen; you're going to America for *seven* days, aren't you?' The enormous significance of Ezekiel 3:6 as the central verse of the whole chapter was still to become clear, but it was true, I was going to America for *seven* days. I welcomed the confirmation from him and the scripture reference to 'seven days'.

I was starting to look at Ezekiel 3. The Lord had got my attention!

Two other areas were bothering me at that time. Firstly, I was waiting upon the Lord for a check I had received on one popular 'signs and wonders' ministry coming into Britain from America. I learned that its outreach to Britain was styled in a way used to describe the New Age movement in America. Secondly, techniques involved with 'Inner Healing' were bothering my spirit more and more. I had been so much involved with visualisation while 'searching' in the occult realm that I couldn't fail to be aware of it as it cropped up in one or another Christian ministry. In the occult we achieved a great deal through imagery, visualisation and imagination. It was clear to me that my walk with Jesus had to be a walk in *faith*. That didn't involve a crucifix or even a picture of Jesus, and it didn't mean a 'Jesus' conjured up in my imagination. I didn't walk with Jesus in my imagination but in faith, and the Lord confirmed to me by His word that *'every imagination of the thoughts of his* (man's) *heart was only evil continually.'* (Genesis 6:5)

With regard to the 'signs and wonders' teacher, the 'inner healing' author and the 'faith' teacher, I knew how possible it was even in a fine Bible-based ministry to hold on to occult ideas or to include new ones. I knew of John's warning against antichrists:

179

'Who is a liar but he that denieth that Jesus is the Christ? He is antichrist, that denieth the Father and the Son' (1 John 2:22).

Certainly we didn't have that here, but I knew that the foundation or root of the teaching had to be considered. Did God or Satan use the technique first? Although similar methods are used by known occult healers where the occult manifestation is demonic nevertheless, with the gifts of the Holy Spirit the manifestation has to be of God, confirmed by His discernment so that we might 'test the spirits' and be certain.

When I travelled to the United States to spend seven days with one of the Christian New Age researchers, the name of the 'faith' teacher was still impressed upon me, but also and more particularly, one 'Inner Healing' author and the 'Signs and Wonders' teacher were firmly on my heart. The scripture the Lord gave me was:

> *'Even him, whose coming is after the working of Satan with all power and signs and lying wonders,*
> *And with all deceivableness of unrighteousness in them that perish; because they received not the love of the truth, that they might be saved.*
> *And for this cause God shall send them strong delusion, that they should believe a lie:*
> *That they all might be damned who believed not the truth, but had pleasure in unrighteousness.*

(2 Thessalonians 2:9–12)

As soon as I arrived in the U.S. and started sharing with my host it became clear my attention there would be directed, not mainly to the devilish devices of the enemy for these last days in the New Age movement itself but to the seeds from it sown to bring about the apostasy (or falling away) of believers. I found there the confirmation for the witness I had in my spirit to the message of the 'Inner Healing' author and to the techniques seen in that sort of ministry more and more in these days. I found the confirmation too for the witness I had about lack of discernment in the 'signs and wonders' ministry the Lord had been pointing out to me.

As for my favourite 'Faith' teacher, I was given one of his American tapes which seemed to put the whole subject into the perspective given me by my friend back home. I had heard the ministry live for a full series of teaching over several days. I had heard English tapes and read the regular mailings, but now I was to hear a tape that astonished me. I could hardly believe my ears:'. . . You don't have a god in you. You *are* one.' What *did* he mean? I knew the Holy Spirit who lived with me and who indeed *was* in me (John 14:17). I knew I was created to have a relationship with God and not to be 'as God' (Genesis 3:5).

Ezekiel chapter three came alive. I had not been sent to a people of obscure speech and difficult language 'but to the house of Israel' (Ezekiel 3:5). Not to the New Agers whose esoteric language could be obscure indeed. Not to the church-going unbelievers whose rituals could be equally difficult. I was going not only to those believers not alert to what is going on in the New Age, but it seemed I was also coming into a conflict of view on some important foundational and fundamental questions with some of those whose teaching had blessed me enormously and for whom I still had a very high personal regard. Certainly I wasn't being sent to 'peoples whose words I would not be able to understand'. Those were the words of Ezekiel 3:6, the verse I had been given back in England.

The Bible I had in America was the N.I.V. and I read in verse nine:

> *'I will make your forehead like the hardest stone, harder than flint. Do not be afraid of them or terrified by them, though they are a rebellious house.'*

I saw my countrymen in exile as the teachers from America who I had listened to (verse 11) and I sat among them for seven days – overwhelmed (verse 15). Indeed I felt overwhelmed by what seemed like error among those who were responsible for so much of the teaching that comes to Britain. I read on to verse seventeen. The Lord had given my host the same scripture for her ministry, and after seven days overwhelmed I received the Word of the Lord (verse 16).

Son of man, I have made you a watchman for the house of Israel; so
'*Son of man, I have made you a watchman for the house of Israel: so*
hear the word I speak, and give them warning from me.' (verse 17)

God called Ezekiel to be a watchman to the house of
Israel in order to warn them of the coming judgment
(Ezekiel 3: 15–21). In Old Testament times a watchman's
job was to keep a keen eye open for attacks coming up on
the horizon outside, and to watch out for fires, riots and
disturbances from within. Ezekiel's main task seems to have
been as a watchman to warn of the imminent judgment of
God upon Israel. He could see it on the horizon. In this
regard Ezekiel must have appeared more gloomy and
critical than those false prophets who failed in their
responsibility to warn Israel. Are these not to be found
among Christians today just as they existed among the Jews
who Ezekiel wrote about? At the end of my stay in America
God seemed to be saying very clearly they *were* to be found
among us.

I waited in the airport hotel for my plane to London. I
read on to verse 22:

'*The hand of the Lord was upon me there, and he said to me, "Get
up and go out to the plain, and there I will speak to you."*'

The Lord really did speak most clearly on the plane! In the
seat next to mine was the man charged with distributing the
teaching materials in the UK for the very 'Signs and
Wonders' ministry about which the Lord had been
speaking all week. In my cabin bag I had hundreds of pages
of that ministry's material, and I had a copy of the New Age
book bearing the same title as the Ministry in the UK.
Later, through the post, I received unexpectedly from him
even more material to provide still further confirmation of
my original discernment. The author of the 'Inner Healing'
book had also seldom been out of my mind during my stay.
My plans had been made in regard to that situation, and the
key was to be in my next trip to be made immediately upon

my arrival home. However the Lord saw it differently and He was to put a brake on my plans. I hadn't reckoned with verse 25 where it said that God would tie me with ropes so I couldn't go out among the people. First I was responsible for leaving my book of new addresses in the seat pocket of the Boeing 747. Secondly, and at about the same time, my house was being burgled. I arrived home to be first on the scene. That kept me from the next conference and from making an approach to the author of the 'Inner Healing' book. Satan's forces had been at work, but as had happened so often, God used that for His purposes so that His will would be done. The Lord was having His way with me and I read verse 26:

> '*I will make you tongue silent so you are unable to rebuke them, though they are a rebellious house.*'

And finally I read verse 27:

> '*But when I speak to you, I will open your mouth and you shall say to them, "This is what the sovereign Lord says." Whoever will listen let him listen, and whoever will refuse let him refuse; for they are a rebellious house.*'

I *had* written about health care in the New Age in my book 'Understanding Alternative Medicine'. Now I had gone to America in the course of getting a wider perspective of the New Age for writing about the New Age. However first and foremost I received clear confirmation of the occult invasion of Christian ministries. We are today seeing what has been called the 'Seduction of Christianity'.

In America the Lord seemed to show me ministry after ministry where there was emphasis on psychology and what *Man* can do. I found ministries preaching the gospel, not of Jesus, but of self-esteem. Others employed techniques of Inner Healing that were found in the occult realm. Another focused on Jesus but also on signs and wonders. Certainly signs and wonders are for today but our focus has to be upon *Jesus*. I could see a terrific move back to biblical signs and wonders. They are scriptural but I was concerned about a 'signs and wonders *movement*' and any *focus* upon them. I could see also that positive confession was scriptural. Salvation, including the healing and wholeness is, according to Romans 10:10, to be confessed with the mouth. That is no basis for a 'positive confession *movement*'.

I was exposing the works of the devil so it is understandable that many reminded *me* of the need to focus on Jesus. They are right. The Lord shifted my focus also from signs and wonders, from positive confession, from techniques of inner healing and from a focus on what this or that leading Christian teacher was saying. He cautioned me through the examples of the miracle ministries and movements, like the Latter Rain Movement of 1948 which took the attention off Jesus and opened the door to occult influence.

While in the U.S.A. the current issue of one big-circulation Christian magazine came into my hands. It was an issue devoted to defending charges of its similarity to the New Age, and the magazine was now the vehicle of one well-known minister who was in his eighties. He had been involved with recognised important ministries and his books had included classics, but, as Dave Hunt, a recognised cult expert, and T. A. McMahon were to confirm in their book 'The Seduction of Christianity' published three months after my visit, the ministry now looked more like Hinduism than Christianity. The Lord had not sent me, as I had believed, to take a look at a New Age movement *outside* the Church – '*not to many peoples of obscure speech and difficult language*' (Ezekiel 3:6) – but to take a look at what was being called the Seduction of Christianity, the invasion of New Age ideas *into* the Church. That at-first-obscure-half-a-sentence in Ezekiel 3:6 given to me by the Lord in advance of the visit was now very clear. I was not to be so much concerned with the New

Age scene and the obscure and even esoteric language that could be found there, nor yet with the professing Church and its often-obscure rituals. I was sent to take a different perspective of the ministries I already knew, including ministries the Lord had already used to teach me — ministries which were part of the charismatic renewal, and whose language I *did* understand.

Paul warned the Thessalonians of the 'falling away' (the apostasy of the Church):

> *'Let no man deceive you by any means: for that day shall not come'* (referring to the 'day of Christ') *except there come a falling away first, and that man of sin be revealed, the son of perdition . . .* (they) *perish because they received not the love of the truth, that they might be saved.'*

> *And for this cause God shall send them strong delusion, that they should believe a lie:*

> *That they will might be damned who believed not the truth, but had pleasure in unrighteousness.*

> (2 Thess 2:3, 10–12)

It is widely believed in the body of Christ that we are in the very end of the end-times. Many look to Jesus' return. But first there must be the son of perdition (the antichrist). And before that, Paul tells us, there must be a falling away.

Back from America, and with the initial dust settled, I resolved to get back into the scriptures. I read and re-read Ezekiel chapters two and three. Ezekiel was cautioned not to rebel against the Lord's message as Israel would. Ezekial had to hear the message, accept it, and having thoroughly understood it, to proclaim it whether or not Israel wanted to hear it.

Given a knowledge of God's word and His discernment we are able to identify the counterfeit and be alert to all the error and wrong doctrine that Satan would seek to bring before each one of us. The message for me was there in the first verse. It pointed to the word of God. I had to **'eat the scroll'** and **'fill my stomach'** with it (Ezekiel 3:1).

20

In Conclusion

Back from America I had to get deeper into my Bible. I had to eat that scroll and fill my stomach with it. Indeed my whole story is a testimony that the Bible is an exciting book and that the Word of God is true. I didn't know that when I stepped forward in faith on Sunday 7th March 1982 in a Pentecostal Church. However I did what Jesus required in order that I would be saved. It is the same for all men.

1. I stepped forward in faith with such faith as I then had.

2. I repented of my sin.

3. I asked Jesus to fill my life.

The blind that Satan had before me for the whole of my life was lifted and I then began to see the truth found only in the Bible, which God continues to reveal to me. I had been born a sinner. I only knew that when I stepped out and became born-again. As I stepped out I didn't know Jesus had actually said:

'Verily, verily, I say unto thee, except a man be born again, he cannot see the kingdom of God.'

(John 3:3)

We receive Jesus *by faith*. We walk with Jesus *by faith*.

The important step for those who are not sure they know Jesus

Perhaps you thought you had to be good in some way in order to become a Christian. Or perhaps you thought your christening, confirmation or churchgoing was the answer. These are Satan's lies and they are *not* the answer. The answer is to believe in Jesus and ask Him into your life.

If you want Jesus to come into your life you can pray this prayer—carefully from your heart. You can also pray this prayer if you are not sure you have Jesus in your Life. It can be a rededication of your life to Him:

> **Jesus,** I believe you are the Son of God, you died on the cross bearing the guilt and the penalty of my sin, and God raised you from the dead.
> **Jesus,** I have sinned by my thoughts, words and actions. I have cut myself off from God. My own efforts will not save me.
> **Jesus,** I am sorry for my sins and I repent.
> **Jesus,** I give my life back to you.
> **Jesus,** I ask you to come into my life
> —as my saviour to cleanse me
> —as my Lord to control me
> —as my friend to be with me
> **Jesus,** I will be obedient to you.
> **Jesus,** you never said it would be easy to follow you but I want to bring every part of my life (work, friendships, money, time) under your control.
> **Jesus,** I can now thank you that you *have* come into my life and I *am* born again.

You are now at the start of a new life. It doesn't matter how old you are or how you *feel*.

1. Read the Bible, and God will speak to you through it.
2. Talk with Jesus as you would with a friend; and pray.
3. Worship in fellowship with others.
4. Witness to others, and tell someone *now* that you are a Christian.

God is true to His word

God is the God of His Word. Jesis is the Word and by Him the world was made. He gave us freewill. We only have to take Him at His word. By His word He has many gifts to lavish upon us. His word says He has for us more than ever we could ask or think.

If you have any questions about the New Age the authors would be pleased to hear from you. Please write to Bury House, Clows Top, Kidderminster, Worcs. DY14 9HX, England.

Other Books by Roy Livesey

UNDERSTANDING ALTERNATIVE MEDICINE –
Health Care in the New Age

* a Christian perspective of New Age health care
* an exposé of the occult explosion in holistic healing
* a plea for discernment

222 pages   £2.95

Marshall, Morgan & Scott (Life Changing Series)/
New Wine Press, 1985

UNDERSTANDING THE NEW AGE – Who Rules the
World

* discerning man's focus upon himself and the creation
* an exposé of Satan's secret rulers on earth
* a plea for discernment in the Church

New Wine Press   (published May 1986)

Trade Orders: New Wine Press, PO Box 17, Chichester,
                  PO20 6YB, England.

Personal Orders: Bury House Christian Books, Clows Top,
                  Kidderminster, Worcs. DY14 9HX,
                  England.